# JOURNAL FOR THE STUDY OF THE OLD TESTAMENT
## SUPPLEMENT SERIES
# 179

*Editors*
David J.A. Clines
Philip R. Davies

*Executive Editor*
John Jarick

*Editorial Board*
Richard J. Coggins, Alan Cooper, Tamara C. Eskenazi,
J. Cheryl Exum, John Goldingay, Robert P. Gordon,
Norman K. Gottwald, Andrew D.H. Mayes, Carol Meyers,
Patrick D. Miller

Sheffield Academic Press

# Time and Place
# in Deuteronomy

## J.G. McConville
## and
## J.G. Millar

Journal for the Study of the Old Testament
Supplement Series 179

For Fiona and Helen

Copyright © 1994 Sheffield Academic Press

Published by
Sheffield Academic Press Ltd
Mansion House
19 Kingfield Road
Sheffield, S11 9AS
England

Typeset by Sheffield Academic Press
and
Printed on acid-free paper in Great Britain
by Bookcraft
Midsomer Norton, Somerset

British Library Cataloguing in Publication Data

A catalogue record for this book is available
from the British Library

ISBN 1-85075-494-2

# CONTENTS

PREFACE

The authors of the present volume met in Oxford while Millar was researching for his DPhil and McConville teaching at Wycliffe Hall. Professor John Barton, as the former's supervisor, asked McConville to act informally as an additional reader. Early in our studies together it became obvious that we were developing very similar ideas about the subject of time and place in Deuteronomy. McConville was working on a monograph whose interest focused on the altar-law, taking further a thesis offered in a previous volume in the present series (*Law and Theology in Deuteronomy*, JSOTSup, 33), but which would set that study in the broader context of relevant themes in the whole book. Millar was studying the topic in the context of his thesis: 'The Ethics of Deuteronomy: An Exegetical and Theological Study of the Book of Deuteronomy'. It seemed entirely natural to combine our efforts and make the common statement that constitutes the present volume.

The work is unusual, we think, in that, though co-authored, it is a synthetic argument, and thus properly a 'monograph'. While Millar has written on the 'framework' and McConville on the 'code', the whole argument is as from both.

We are grateful to the editors of Journal for the Study of the Old Testament Supplement Series for accepting the volume into the series. From McConville's point of view, it complements the argument he offered in the work mentioned above, and he is therefore glad that this one finds a place in the same series. We are grateful too to Professor Barton for encouraging the enterprise, for his care and attentiveness as a supervisor, and for reading the whole work presented here and making important suggestions.

We are also grateful to each other. Apart from sharing a place of origin (in Ulster), and initials (confusingly), we have been able to share our enthusiasm for the book of Deuteronomy, and we hope a lasting friendship, though time and place have already changed—which is a large part of our point.

# ABBREVIATIONS

| | |
|---|---|
| AB | Anchor Bible |
| AnBib | Analecta biblica |
| BBB | Bonner biblische Beiträge |
| BETL | Bibliotheca ephemeridum theologicarum lovaniensium |
| BEvT | Beiträge zur evangelischen Theologie |
| *Bib* | *Biblica* |
| *BibLeb* | *Bibel und Leben* |
| BibOr | Biblica et orientalia |
| BJS | Brown Judaic Studies |
| BWANT | Beiträge zur Wissenschaft vom Alten und Neuen Testament |
| *BZ* | *Biblische Zeitschrift* |
| BZAW | Beihefte zur *ZAW* |
| *CBQ* | *Catholic Biblical Quarterly* |
| ConBOT | Coniectanea biblica, Old Testament |
| *EstBíb* | *Estudios bíblicos* |
| ICC | International Critical Commentary |
| *Int* | *Interpretation* |
| *JBL* | *Journal of Biblical Literature* |
| JSOTSup | *Journal for the Study of the Old Testament*, Supplement Series |
| JSPSup | *Journal for the Study of the Pseudepigrapha*, Supplement Series |
| NCB | New Century Bible |
| NICNT | New International Commentary on the New Testament |
| NICOT | New International Commentary on the Old Testament |
| *NKZ* | *Neue kirchliche Zeitschrift* |
| OBT | Overtures to Biblical Theology |
| OTL | Old Testament Library |
| *RB* | *Revue biblique* |
| SBLDS | SBL Dissertation Series |
| SBS | Stuttgarter Bibelstudien |
| SJ | Studia judaica |
| TOTC | Tyndale Old Testament Commentaries |
| *TynBul* | *Tyndale Bulletin* |
| *VT* | *Vetus Testamentum* |
| VTSup | *Vetus Testamentum*, Supplements |
| WBC | Word Biblical Commentary |
| WMANT | Wissenschaftliche Monographien zum Alten und Neuen Testament |
| *ZAW* | *Zeitschrift für die alttestamentliche Wissenschaft* |
| *ZDPV* | *Zeitschrift des deutschen Palästina-Vereins* |

# INTRODUCTION

The essays in the present volume are concerned with Deuteronomy's stance towards the programme of the Josianic reform. As such, they are a contribution first and foremost to the theological interpretation of Deuteronomy, and an exercise in Old Testament theology. At the same time they raise questions of methodology in the criticism of the book. The intimate relationship between these two kinds of issues needs no demonstration, nor indeed does the importance of Deuteronomy in relation to each. Both in the theology of the Old Testament and in the annals of modern Old Testament criticism, Deuteronomy occupies an unrivalled place.

The study of Deuteronomy, however, is beset by what D.L. Christensen has called 'the current methodological quandary' in its study.[1] The older style of literary criticism of Steuernagel and others has been overlaid by form criticism (von Rad), then the tradition criticism of Noth's theory of the Deuteronomist, and finally an approach that owes more to rhetorical criticism, in which the stylistic studies of Lohfink have been prominent.[2]

The dominant force in the field is probably redaction criticism. Wellhausen's belief that Deuteronomy originally consisted of a law-code which was subsequently provided with introductions as well as concluding materials has given way to a model of more organic growth which took its stimulus from Noth's belief that Deuteronomy 1–3 constituted the introduction to the Deuteronomic History (DtH).[3] Noth's

---

1.  D.L. Christensen, *Deuteronomy 1–11* (WBC 6a; Dallas: Word, 1991), p. xlix.

2.  The survival of literary criticism in tradition-critical interpretations is evidenced in the treatments of Deut. 12 by M. Rose, *Der Ausschliesslichkeitsanspruch Jahwes* (BWANT, 106; Stuttgart: Kohlhammer, 1975), pp. 97-98; G. Seitz, *Redaktionsgeschichtliche Studien zum Deuteronomium* (BWANT, 93; Stuttgart: Kohlhammer, 1971), pp. 212-14.

3.  M. Noth, *The Deuteronomistic History* (JSOTSup, 15; Sheffield: JSOT Press, 1981).

idea of Deuteronomistic revisions to the original Deuteronomy was pressed further by G. Minette de Tillesse, who saw in the feature of number-change in second-person address a criterion for discerning different strata,[4] and subsequently in a number of works which have sought to identify successive Deuteronomistic levels.[5] H.D. Preuss, in his compendious review of modern research, states his view that future study of Deuteronomy is bound to proceed along the route of an *Ergänzungshypothese*,[6] that is, in line with developments in tradition criticism.

One implication of the advance of redaction criticism is the increasing elusiveness of the 'original' Deuteronomy (*Urdeuteronomium, Urdt*).[7] Indeed, the distinction, in literary-critical terms, between 'framework' and 'code' is no longer as significant as it once was. The laws too are held to have been subject to Deuteronomic expansion.[8] A consequence of this concept of gradual accretion to Deuteronomy is that the relationship of the book to Josiah's reform has become less clear than it was thought to be in the heyday of literary criticism. Form criticism too played its part in this disjunction, with its attempt to locate the original Deuteronomy in a northern, cultic milieu.[9]

Nevertheless, in most critical interpretation, Deuteronomy remains firmly wedded to the seventh century and even to Josiah. Attempts to trace the growth from pre-Deuteronomic material through the Deuteronomic stage to Deuteronomistic redaction almost invarariably move along a trajectory from Josiah (or somewhat before him) to the

---

4.    G. Minette de Tillesse, 'Sections "Tu" et Sections "Vous" dans le Deutéronome', VT 12 (1982), pp. 29-87.

5.    E.g. S. Mittmann, *Deuteronomium 1.1–6.3 literarkritisch und traditions-geschichtlich untersucht* (BZAW, 139; Berlin: de Gruyter, 1975); Rose, *Ausschliesslichkeitsanspruch*.

6.    H.D. Preuss, *Deuteronomium* (Erträge der Forschung, 164; Darmstadt: Wissenschaftliche Buchgesellschaft, 1982), pp. 42-43.

7.    Preuss, *Deuteronomium*.

8.    R.P. Merendino, *Das deuteronomische Gesetz: Eine literarkritische, gattungs- und überlieferungsgeschichtliche Untersuchung zu Dt. 12–26* (BBB, 31; Bonn: Hanstein, 1969).

9.    G. von Rad, 'The Form-Critical Problem of the Hexateuch', in *The Problem of the Hexateuch and other Essays* (London: SCM Press, 1984), pp. 27-28, 36-38; cf. *idem*, *Studies in Deuteronomy* (London: SCM Press, 1953), p. 14. See also J.G. McConville, *Grace in the End: A Study in Deuteronomic Theology* (Studies in Old Tesament Biblical Theology; Carlisle: Paternoster, 1993), pp. 20-24, for discussion.

exile.[10] To take an example, M. Rose traces the Yahwistic claim to exclusiveness in the monarchy period. In his view, the idea of election, focused on the people, existed from the time of the early monarchy, as Judah struggled for its identity over against Canaan.[11] This pre-Deuteronomic concept gave way under the pressure of events—the integrity of the historic people having been lost—and was replaced by the Deuteronomic focus of the election theology on the chosen place following the deliverance of Jerusalem in 701 BC.[12] The longer and shorter forms of the altar-law then reflect Josianic and post-Josianic developments of election theology.[13]

As is clear from this one example, such reconstructions involve judgments of one sort or another about the character of the Deuteronomic programme. Rose's redaction criticism presupposes that that programme promotes the interests of the Jerusalem sanctuary. This, however, is debated in scholarly interpretation, some scholars proposing that Deuteronomy has just such a positive view of the Jerusalem religious establishment, while others believe it is critical.[14] The debate, which is charted more fully below, affects not only Deuteronomy, but also DtH. Cross's two-edition theory of the composition of DtH has linked it firmly, in its original form, with the promotion of the Reform.[15] Where a single-edition theory is held, however, a more critical stance in relation to Jerusalem and monarchy is implied.[16] It need hardly be said that interpretations of Deuteronomy and DtH tend to influence each other,

---

10. A fuller treatment of modern criticism and interpretation is found below, in McConville's essay.

11. Rose, *Ausschliesslichkeitsanspruch*, pp. 94-95.

12. Rose, *Ausschliesslichkeitsanspruch*, pp. 96-97.

13. Rose, *Ausschliesslichkeitsanspruch*, pp. 97-100.

14. For example, M. Weinfeld locates Deuteronomy close to the royal court; *Deuteronomy and the Deuteronomic School* (Oxford: Clarendon, 1972), pp. 161-64; cf. *idem*, 'The Emergence of the Deuteronomic Movement; The Historical Antecedents', in *Das Deuteronomium: Entstehung, Gestalt und Botschaft* (ed. N. Lohfink; Leuven: Leuven University Press, 1985), pp. 76-98; O. Bächli, *Israel und die Völker* (Zürich: Zwingli Verlag, 1962), pp. 186ff. Contrast, however, J. Halbe, 'Gemeinschaft die Welt unterbricht', *Das Deuteronomium* (ed. Lohfink), pp. 57-59. And see fuller discussion in McConville, *Grace in the End*, pp. 24-33.

15. F.M. Cross, *Canaanite Myth and Hebrew Epic* (Cambridge, MA: Harvard University Press, 1973), pp. 274-89.

16. As in the case of Noth's seminal work, *The Deuteronomistic History*; see also McConville, 'Narrative and Meaning in the Books of Kings', *Bib* 70 (1989), pp. 31-49.

and Cross's work has both drawn on and in turn supported a 'Josianic' interpretation of the former.

At this point it is in place to notice the relative newcomer in Deuteronomy studies, namely rhetorical or stylistic criticism, spearheaded by N. Lohfink. Lohfink's studies have presented a formidable challenge at least to some of the well-tried techniques of redaction criticism in Deuteronomy, especially the use of the number-change in second-person address.[17] Yet in his own way he also engages in redaction criticism, and understands the emergence of Deuteronomy in the context of Josiah's reform, allowing indeed for the assimilation of both northern and southern elements.[18]

In fact the question about the relationship between synchronic and diachronic study of Deuteronomy remains unresolved. The Leuven volume on Deuteronomy, edited by Lohfink, represents the tensions that exist. In it, L. Perlitt reaffirms the primacy of diachronic methods, expressly rejecting R. Polzin's structuralist approach, while Vermeylen's contribution (diachronic) seems to inhabit a different world from that of Christensen.[19]

The present study is concerned with the relationship between synchronic study and historical questions. It is not a strictly theoretical study, but rather asks the question how a synchronic reading might affect the central historical questions. That is, does it have a bearing on the crucial issue of the relation of the book to Josiah's reform? In this discussion, the altar-law (Deut. 12.5 etc.) still plays a major role, as a key link between the book and the account of the reform in 2 Kings 22–23. Our study, therefore, is conceived as a contextual investigation of the altar-law. That is, it will examine its context in the book in the widest sense, exploring links between it and themes in the framework. In this enterprise, we are in line with one of the trends in Deuteronomy-studies

17. N. Lohfink, *Das Hauptgebot* (Rome: Biblical Institute Press, 1963), especially pp. 239ff.

18. *Idem*, 'Die Bundesurkunde des Königs Josias: Eine Frage an die Deuteronomiumsforschung', *Bib* 44 (1963), pp. 261-88, 461-98.

19. Perlitt, 'Deut. 1–3 im Streit der exegetischen Methoden', in *Das Deuteronomium* (ed. Lohfink), pp. 149-63. Contrast R. Polzin, *Moses and the Deuteronomist* (New York: Seabury, 1980); J. Vermeylen, 'Les sections narratives de Deut. 5–11 et leur relation à Ex 19–34', *Das Deuteronomium* (ed. Lohfink), pp. 174-207; D.L. Christensen, 'Form and Structure in Deuteronomy 1–11', *ibid*, pp. 135-44. Christensen's recent commentary develops his 'symphonic' reading of Deuteronomy: *Deuteronomy 1–11*.

which we have observed, namely the tendency to find links between the 'code' and the 'framework', and the breakdown of the belief that the two entities can be separated cleanly from each other in historical-critical terms. We also develop a line of argument that was proposed in an earlier work of McConville's, where formal and thematic similarities were shown between Deuteronomy 7 and Deuteronomy 12.[20]

The altar-law has so often been treated as a problem to be solved (which place?) that thematic questions that arise in connection with it have often been missed. In fact, we believe, it begs to be discussed in terms of Deuteronomic themes, most obviously those of time and space (or place): 'in the *land which the LORD...has given you to possess all the days that you live upon the earth...*you *shall seek* the *place* (Deut. 12.1, 5). As topics of scholarly discussion in Deuteronomy these are not new in themselves. However, they have not yet been properly brought into conjunction with the criticism of the altar-law. In what follows, Millar examines the themes of time and place in chs. 1–11, 27–34, and McConville's study of the altar-law builds on his findings. The method of proceeding is primarily rhetorical-critical, or synchronic. The aim is to see the broad picture before trying to interpret the parts. This, we are aware, is somewhat controversial, yet in our view the constraints put upon synchronic reading by, for example, Perlitt, are such that synchronic reading might never actually be done. This means that, while a number of individual critical points will be taken up along the way, there is no systematic attempt here to deal with every literary-critical issue. Yet we believe that the results of the study have important consequences for the reading of Deuteronomy, in terms of both literary and historical criticism. Those results suggest that Deuteronomy as a whole undermines rather than promotes the belief that God's purposes for his people were permanently realized in Jerusalem, or any other place. The perspective on Deuteronomy thus offered stands in contrast in particular to the recent tendency to see the book as 'statist'.

20. McConville, *Law and Theology*, pp. 59-64.

LIVING AT THE PLACE OF DECISION:
TIME AND PLACE IN THE FRAMEWORK OF DEUTERONOMY

J.G. Millar

*Introduction*

The framework of Deuteronomy, while containing a wide variety of literary forms, is held together by a common preoccupation with the ethical and theological decisions facing Israel on the verge of the land, and beyond that in the land itself.

One of the features which link the disparate elements is a consistent use of temporal and spatial ideas to sharpen the demands made of Israel by Yahweh. Chapters 1–11 and 27–34 show Israel to be on a journey between successive places of significance in the national life. The journey begins in Egypt, moves on to Horeb, and then via Kadesh Barnea to Moab. This movement provides the core of the opening three chapters. At each point Yahweh instructs Israel in obedience.

The Deuteronomist, however, is not simply interested in retelling the history of the nation. This material is carefully phrased to show that Israel must remember the lessons of the past and continually apply them to the future—the key to acting properly at Moab, for example, lies in learning from the mistakes of Kadesh Barnea.

The identification of present and past experience is developed in ch. 4, where Israel is faced with a recapitulation of the events of Horeb, rather than Kadesh Barnea. This clearly has much more far-reaching consequences for the interpretation of the book. From the general principles drawn from the theophany at Horeb in ch. 4, ch. 5 moves on to a specific identification of the content of the revelation at Horeb with the Mosaic preaching at Moab. The effect is to gather up every significant moment in Israel's past experience in the present dilemma at Moab.

The parenesis in chs. 6–11 builds on and expands this use of time and place to emphasize the requisite of obedience in response to the continuing revelation of Yahweh. Part of its contribution is to introduce a future perspective to the ethical agenda, asking how Israel is to obey when Moab itself is only a distant memory. The key to the future is described in terms of obedience in the present informed by remembrance of the past.

In the conclusion to the book (chs. 27–34) this extrapolation of the present to future situations becomes the dominant theme. The inevitable consequence of disobedience will be expulsion from the land, with a renewed commitment to obey based on a rediscovery of the past the only way to restoration. Even the final historical details, and ancient poetry, utilize time and place for such an overtly hortatory purpose.

The theology of Deuteronomy does not begin and end with ideas of time and place. Together, however, they form a prominent device used to illustrate the central concerns of the author(s). The recognition that temporal and spatial concepts are carefully arranged and used to serve a parenetic agenda provides a valuable hermeneutical tool in interpreting the framework of the book, and has ramifications which influence not only the understanding of the altar law in ch. 12, but beyond to the place of Deuteronomy within the scheme of Old Testament history.

### 1. *Time and Place in Chapters 1–3:*
### *The Introduction of the Journey of Israel*

It is not easy to decide what to do with the first three chapters of Deuteronomy. The material contained here appears to be radically different from almost everything which follows in the rest of the book. Chapters 1–3 are Mosaic speech, yet do not share in the rich rhetoric of chs. 6–11. Nor is legal material prominent. There is no sign of ancient fragments of poetic material. Rather we have a selective rehearsal of the Wilderness years and journey to the edge of the land of Canaan. This puzzle has given rise to many literary-critical theories, none of which has gained universal acceptance.

While there have been numerous attempts to account for the literary relationship of these chapters with the rest of the book and other biblical material (notably the Numbers version of the Exodus and the Deuteronomistic conquest tradition), any examination of the *theological* concerns has been conspicuous only by its absence. In this section I shall attempt to demonstrate that many of the difficulties pointed out by historical criticism find their meaning in the Deuteronomic theological agenda. The pointed retelling of the history of Israel is essential to set the context for what follows. The function of these chapters is to bring Israel to the place of decision on the edge of the land. In doing so the categories of 'Time' and 'Place' are introduced as the bedrock of the parenetic material which follows. Deuteronomy 1–3 cannot be excised from the rest of the book—without these chapters the ethical and theological vigour of the Mosaic preaching would be reduced to abstract moralizing.

*History of Interpretation*
Such has been the impact of the first part of Martin Noth's *Überlieferungsgeschichtliche Studien*,[1] that the interpretation of these chapters can be divided into 'pre-' and 'post-Noth'.

In the nineteenth and early twentieth centuries the opinion that the first three chapters were to be separated from the rest of the book was proposed and quickly gathered supporters including Wellhausen and Steuernagel.[2] Little agreement was reached, however, on how to account for the differences in language, tone and concerns. The theory of a 'double introduction' to the Deuteronomic law, regarding chs. 1–3 as a preface to 5–11, which in turn was the preface to the law, was the most commonly held view at a time when no real consensus had been reached. It was in this context that Noth produced his thesis, which brought about a complete paradigm shift in Deuteronomic Studies.

Noth's most radical innovation was the suggestion that chs. 1–3 have no link whatsoever with the Deuteronomic law, but serve as the introduction to the Deuteronomistic history.[3] Therefore any connection with the rest of the book of Deuteronomy is an artificial one. He supports this position by arguing that the historical details included, in sharp contrast to chs. 5–11, are not used to urge a particular ethical course of action

---

1. (Tübingen: Max Niemayer Verlag, 2nd edn, 1957); ET *The Deuteronomistic History* (JSOTSup, 15; Sheffield: JSOT Press, 1981).

2. The suggestion was first made in P. Kleinert, *Untersuchungen zur alttestamentlichen Rechts- und Literaturgeschichte. I. Das Deuteronomium und der Deuteronomiker* (Leipzig: Velhagen & Klasing, 1872). S.R. Driver was one of the few to maintain that chs. 1–11 should be regarded as a unity—see *A Critical and Exegetical Commentary on Deuteronomy* (ICC; Edinburgh: T. & T. Clark, 3rd edn, 1901).

3. 'One quickly finds persuasive evidence that 1.1–4.43 has nothing in common with the Deuteronomic law but is directly related to the Deuteronomistic history. From this we conclude that Deut. 1–3(4) is not the introduction to the Deuteronomic law but the beginning of the Deuteronomistic historical narrative and that this narrative begins therefore at 1.1' (Noth, *Deuteronomistic History*, p. 29).

upon Israel. For Noth, this material is intended to equip the reader of the Deuteronomistic history with the details needed to understand the narrative which follows. The relevance of these chapters is primarily to the book of Joshua, and not to Deuteronomy itself. This, along with the Deuteronomist's concern to present a 'systematic theological interpretation of history'[4] and a concise chronology of the wilderness experience, explains the inclusion of the Caleb material (cf. Josh. 14.6-14), the Sihon and Og narratives and the traditions concerning the occupation of Transjordan. There are still elements (notably the appointment of judges in 1.9-18) which remain a mystery.

The major tenets of Noth's work have found almost universal acceptance. Recent studies can basically be characterized by how they have modified his findings and have been of the order of adjustments rather than innovations.[5] Some have adopted Noth's position basically unchanged, others have placed more emphasis on the input of the Deuteronomistic school, while others still have sought to differentiate between various (usually early and late) Deuteronomistic redactions. I shall not attempt to discuss all such studies, but rather concentrate on those dealing with the question of sources in chs. 1–3, and the distinctives of the version of Israel's history given here.

Hempel first suggested that it may be possible to separate this section of the text into singular and plural layers.[6] This is, of course, a familiar problem in Deuteronomic studies, but the situation here is somewhat different from that in the rest of the book. The variation is not simply between the second-person singular and plural, but rather the first and second person (singular and plural). Cazelles contends that we have a narrative in the plural augmented by comments in the singular (which he lists as 1.21, 31a, 2.7, 24b, 30b—see also 3.21, 28). Plöger has followed a broadly similar line of inquiry in much greater detail.[7]

---

4.    Noth, *Deuteronomistic History*, p. 52.

5.    See H.D. Preuss, *Deuteronomium* (Erträge der Forschung, 164; Darmstadt: Wissenschaftliche Buchgesellschaft, 1982), p. 77. Such has been the impact of his study that Preuss can say with some justification that 'Wer heute etwas zu Dtn. 1–3 sagt, muss zu dieser These Stellung nehmen bzw (schlicht ausgedrückt) einleuchtend machen, was Dtn. 1–3 sonst noch sein könnten, wenn sie nicht die Einleitungsrede zum DtrG sind'.

6.    See *Die Schichten des Deuteronomiums* (Leipzig: Voigtländer, 1914).

7.    H. Cazelles, 'Passages in the Singular within Discourses in the Plural of Dt. 1–4', *CBQ* 29 (1967), pp. 207-19. J.G. Plöger, *Literarkritische, formgeschicht-*

Plöger sees behind chs. 2 and 3 originally profane accounts of both the journey through the wilderness (the 'Wegbericht') and the subsequent military encounters (the 'Kampfbericht'). These are contained in the 'we' sections of the text.[8] This source (which is reflected uniquely in Deuteronomy) was augmented in several stages. First, a theological significance was imparted to the whole unit through the prefaced speech of Yahweh in 1.6-8. Then speeches in the second-person singular and plural were inserted throughout to ensure the material served the Deuteronomistic purpose.[9] A secondary 'we section' (based around the Sihon and Og narratives) serves to summarize, while the introduction of the land distribution material facilitates a smooth transition to the conquest (as in Noth's reconstruction).[10]

Chapter 1 is treated separately in two stages. In 1.9-18 Plöger discerns the introduction of *statist* concerns, loosely linking the speech of Yahweh in 1.6-8 with the spy narrative, arising from an independent tradition, which follows.[11]

Plöger's careful study has not met with complete acceptance. It has been criticised by Lohfink, in an extensive review article, and also in the lengthy work of Mittmann.[12] It is questionable if the journey material can be so easily separated from the rest of chs. 1–3, and also from the usual Deuteronomistic depiction. Mittmann's disagreement with Plöger, however, goes even deeper than that. He finds a thoroughgoing pre-Deuteronomic plural layer running throughout 1.1–6.3, which was the original introduction to the Deuteronomic law. A singular layer was

---

*liche und stilkritische Untersuchungen zum Deuteronomium* (BBB, 26; Bonn: Peter Hanstein, 1967).

8.  2.1, 8, 13b, 14, 30a, 32-36; 3.1, 3, 8, 12, 29. See also G. von Rad, *Deuteronomy* (OTL; London: SCM Press, 1966).

9.  Plural speeches = 2.2-7, 9-13a, 17, 24. Sing. speeches = 2.31, 3.2 etc. It is interesting that there appears to be little means of separating the singular and plural strands here.

10.  See the land material in the speeches of 1.7, 8, 21, 22, 26, 35; 2.5, 9, 19, 27 etc. The full details of Plöger's analysis are on pp. 20-22 of *Untersuchungen*.

11.  He does not make clear the nature of such a link. The motivation for such statist sentiments arose much later than the original material—'Es ist daher wahrscheinlich, dass die Interpolation daran lag, den Gehorsam gegen "Obrigkeit" und "Gesetz" zu betonen' (*Untersuchungen*, p. 39).

12.  N. Lohfink, in *Bib* 49 (1968), pp. 110-15. S. Mittmann, *Deuteronomium 1.1–6.3 literarkritisch und traditionsgeschichtlich untersucht* (BZAW, 39; Berlin: A. Töpelmann, 1975). See also Preuss, *Deuteronomium*, p. 80.

added which integrated a primitive version of the book with the Pentateuch. The situation was then complicated by the fusion of a further plural layer joining Deuteronomy with Joshua–Kings, and the entangled network completed by an extra singular layer.[13] Even this briefest of summaries of his work betrays some of its weaknesses. It has been heavily criticised as being subjective, using slightly dubious criteria for literary analysis and making extravagant claims for his findings.[14]

Thus neither of the major attempts to provide a literary-critical solution to the problem of these three chapters has been entirely successful. Nor have the several shorter papers aimed at fixing the tradition history (and purpose) of smaller sections of the text proved compelling.[15]

The two most satisfactory pieces of work to emerge in the 'post-Noth' period have been those which have concentrated on the theological rationale behind the presentation of events in Deuteronomy 1–3. Norbert Lohfink, in 'Darstellungskunst und Theologie in Dtn. 1.6-3.29', makes the crucial observation that the absence of explicit theological reflection in this section means that the theology of these verses is only accessible through a recognition of their literary characteristics.[16] The recognition that this material is profoundly theological is a welcome corrective to Noth.

From this starting point Lohfink proceeds to examine the distinctive features of each pericope. He perceives that ch. 1 is suffused with Deuteronomic concerns, particularly that of holy war. It is argued that the source (which is similar or identical to the Numbers material) has been reworked to portray the failures of Israel as preventing embarkation on the holy war, and to emphasize the role of the people (rather than the spies or Moses) in this failure.[17] This can easily be seen in the significance which the sending of the spies (an almost irrelevant detail in

13. Mittmann, *Deuteronomium 1.1–6.3*, p. 170.

14. Mittmann has been heavily criticised by Braulik (see the review in *Bib* 59 [1978], pp. 351-83), and Preuss, *Deuteronomium*, who in turn cites Thiel and Macholz.

15. E.g. J.R. Bartlett, 'Sihon and Og, Kings of the Amorites', *VT* 20 (1970), pp. 257-77; W.A. Sumner, 'Israel's Encounters with Edom, Moab, Ammon, Sihon and Og according to the Deuteronomist', *VT* 18 (1968), pp. 216-28; G.W. Coats, 'Conquest Traditions in the Wilderness Theme', *JBL* 95 (1976), pp. 177-90; J. Van Seters, 'The Conquest of Sihon's Kingdom: A Literary Examination', *JBL* 91 (1972), pp. 182-97.

16. *Bib* 41 (1960), pp. 105-34, esp 106.

17. Compare von Rad, Preuss on these incidents in ch. 1.

Numbers) takes on in this passage. Alongside this he highlights the presence of 'the way' as a *Leitvorstellung* in the spy narrative, which serves to provide a psychological analysis of the belief and unbelief of the Israelites. The function of ch. 1 is both to bring Israel to a point of decision, and to depict the experiences after Kadesh Barnea as an 'Anti-Exodus'.[18]

Lohfink goes further to demonstrate the presence of legal elements in 1.8, and implicitly throughout the chapter, which sets the whole spy narrative in the context of a legal agreement whose effectiveness can be annulled by the disobedience of one party (Israel) and yet can be rejuvenated by the next generation (after a remedial journey, in this case).[19] This is the most promising way of dealing with 1.9-18 that we have yet seen.

In view of the 'Anti-Exodus' motif, and the failings of the first generation, the conquest of Transjordan is presented as a counter-example. Initially a new rhythm of command and execution is established for the ongoing journey of Israel in ch. 2. The occupation of Transjordan is then established as a paradigm for the continuing journey of Israel into and within Canaan itself.

Lohfink maintains his support for Noth's basic thesis throughout.[20] This is despite his continued affirmation that chs. 1–3 introduce and reflect the wider theological concerns of the book of Deuteronomy as a whole—particularly the concern with the holy war (albeit in an inverted form), the journey motif, and the decision facing Israel. The same can be said of Plöger. There seems a basic contradiction here, which may suggest that it is time to challenge one of the sacred cows of the interpretation of Deuteronomy.

Literary-critical analysis of Deuteronomy 1–3 on the lines suggested by Noth's seminal work has provided neither assured results nor a consensus view. The few attempts to examine the theology of these

---

18. 'Diese zeigen sich von dem Punkt an, wo in beiden Erzählungen (viz Num. & Dtn.) der Knoten der Handlung geschürzt ist und die Entscheidungen fallen...Ist Dtn. 1 "ein pervertierter Gotteskrieg", dann ist es noch präziser ein "Anti-Exodus"'; 'Darstellungskunst', p. 119. This latter theme is further developed by W.L. Moran, in 'The End of the Unholy War and the Anti-Exodus', *Bib* 44 (1963), pp. 333-42, with particular reference to 2.14-16.

19. 'Darstellungskunst', pp. 123-25.

20. Parts of his argument (e.g. his explanation of the adaptation of the Mosaic intercession tradition in the spy story as an anticipation of the end of 2 Kings— p. 116) seem classically 'orthodox'.

chapters appear ultimately to be hamstrung by their basic commitment to the Deuteronomistic (rather than Deuteronomic) character of the chapters. It may be that further advance in this area can only come in the wake of a re-evaluation of the basic tenets of Noth's treatment of the text .

Two contentions lie at the heart of Noth's thesis: first, that chs. 1–3 have no real connection with what follows, and secondly, that their 'theological' significance (if it can even be called such) is to be restricted to the level of facilitating the Deuteronomistic chronology to be developed later, and of introducing the characters in a future drama. Both of these assertions are highly dubious. Clearly, if it could be demonstrated that there are conceptual and rhetorical links between chs. 1–3 and the rest of Deuteronomy, and that there is a theological message here which is fundamentally different to the supposed Deuteronomistic programmatic view of history, then Noth's thesis would be seriously undermined.[21] The work of Lohfink, Moran and Plöger seems to point the way to just such an alternative understanding.

In addition to this, the virtually universal commitment to the *Numeruswechsel* as a criterion for literary-critical analysis has come under severe criticism since the days of Noth. Lohfink, in particular, has challenged the indiscriminate use of number-change in this way, arguing that it is often a deliberate device for emphasis.[22] It is especially dubious to use such a method where conventional narrative is punctuated by speeches, interspersed with the narrator's comments and occasional historical flotsam.There seems little reason to insist that the presence of speeches in the second person in the middle of a first person account is an indication of literary compositeness. Nor is the occasional use of the singular necessarily due to editorial processes. In 1.21, 31a; 2.7, 24b, 30b; 3.21, 28 the use of the change of number as a rhetorical

---

21. Noth may be accused of reductionism in his characterisation of alternative views. He argues that since 1-3 has no connection with the 'lawcode' (his view of how 4–11 fit into this is unclear) it must be Deuteronomistic. The only other understanding he countenances is that we have a double introduction. Chs. 1–3 need not be *directly* related to the lawcode to be Deuteronomic.

22. See N. Lohfink, *Das Hauptgebot: Eine Untersuchung literarischer Einleitungsfragen zu Dtn. 5–11* (AnBib, 20; Rome: Pontifical Biblical Institute, 1963), pp. 312ff., and also F. Garcia Lopez, 'Analyse littéraire de Deut. 5–11', *RB* 84 (1977), pp. 481-522 and 85 (1978), pp. 1-49; M. Weinfeld, *Deuteronomy 1–11* (AB; New York: Doubleday, 1990); A.D.H. Mayes, *Deuteronomy* (NCB; Grand Rapids; Eerdmans London: Marshall Morgan & Scott, 1979).

device, whether to engage the attention of the audience or to underline the responsibility of every member of the community, is not only possible, but often demanded.

These conclusions warrant a fresh examination of the text, with a view to investigating the theological concerns of chs. 1–3, if such exist, and the relationship of these chapters to what follows in the rest of the book.

### Interpretation of Deuteronomy 1–3

In accordance with the proposal that chs. 1–3 establish time and place as theological and ethical categories in the book of Deuteronomy, it is possible to consider this material under two broad categories—*places of failure* and *the road to success*. The opening chapter is concerned with places of failure in the experience of Israel. At 2.1 a turning point is reached, and the journey of reversal counters past disappointments and disobedience with a paradigm of success with Yahweh in the occupation of Transjordan.

After the declaration that 'these are the words of Moses', Deuteronomy begins with a salvo of seemingly irrelevant geographical and historical details. These are generally passed over with little more than the briefest of archaeological comment. But it may well be that the author(s) of the book have included these details in the interests of theology rather than archaeology. Fixing the place of Moses' address, and the time, no doubt had the effect of recalling a well-known juncture in national history—this was the day of Israel's decision to enter the land. This was the time and place of Israel's second chance.

Only in this context can the banal parenthesis of 1.2 be seen to make any sense. At first glance it seems extremely odd to encounter such a mundane geographical note here, and commentators struggle to shed any light on it.[23] If, however, the primary purpose of beginning the book in this unexpected way is to draw the reader's attention immediately to the significance of time and place for the message (not simply being a

---

23. I could find no explanation in any of the recent commentaries for the appearance of Kadesh Barnea here—Weinfeld came closest by acknowledging it as a problem and rejecting it as a late gloss—only Keil admitted the possibility of a significance beyond the geographical: 'Moses reminded the people that they had completed the journey from Horeb...to Kadesh in eleven days that he might lead them to lay to heart the events which took place at Kadesh itself'; C.F. Keil, in Keil, and F. Delitzsch, *Commentary on the Old Testament*. I. *The Pentateuch* (ET 1864, repr. Grand Rapids: Eerdmans, 1988), p. 281.

result of gradual accretion of traditional material), then the mist clears a little. The purpose of v. 2 is to bring the national failure at Kadesh Barnea to the forefront of the listener's or reader's mind, in contrast to the response demanded of Israel at Horeb. What follows is then framed as a potential repetition or reparation of an old mistake at a new place— we shall see that Moab is to be understood as both a second Kadesh and a second Horeb. The relative obscurity of the location only serves to highlight the content of the actual decision facing Israel.[24]

Such a significance for time and place is supported by the precise temporal reference in v. 3, suggesting that this was a special moment in the history of Israel. The introduction of Sihon and Og has the effect of underlining the position of this moment on the timeline, and reiterating the possibilities for success despite the previous disaster at Kadesh.[25] The puzzling repetition of the location of Moses' discourse in v. 5 then may be seen not as a quirk of the tradition history of the passage, but as an emphatic affirmation of the importance of time and place in the narrative to follow.[26]

This view of the opening of the book, not surprisingly, finds support in Rabbinic traditions and the Targumim:

> If the Israelites had had the merit, they would have entered the land in all of eleven days' [journey from beginning to end, instead of forty years]. But because they fouled up through their deeds, the Omnipresent turned forty days for them into forty years. [27]
>
> He rebuked them for having sinned in the wilderness and having caused provocation in the plains opposite the Sea of Reeds; at Paran they talked

---

24. This idea of vagueness may find some support in the Deuteronomic preference for Horeb ('waste place') rather than Sinai. See L. Perlitt, 'Horeb und Sinai', *Beiträge zur alttestamentlichen Theologie* (FS W. Zimmerli; ed. H. Donner; Göttingen: Vandenhoeck & Ruprecht, 1977), pp. 303-22, esp. 307-8.

25. See the discussions of Moran, 'Anti-Exodus', and Lohfink, 'Darstellungskunst'.

26. Noth sees this as an interpolation which disturbs the syntax and 'contrary to Dtr.'s intention mentions the law at this early stage and hence sees Dt. 1–3(4) as a speech introducing the law' (*Deuteronomistic History*, p. 46 n. 3). This is unsatisfactory, since the use of 'torah' in this context does not demand that chs. 1–3 is an intoduction to the law as such (see G. Braulik, 'Die Ausdrücke für Gesetz im Buch Deuteronomium', *Bib* 51 [1970], pp. 39-66; for other examples of asyndeton see GKC §120g, h.

27. Sifre to Deuteronomy II.1.E; see J. Neusner, *Sifre to Deuteronomy*, I, II (BJS, 98, 101; Atlanta: Scholars Press, 1987).

irreverently about the Manna, and at Haseroth they caused provocation about the meat, and because they made the golden calf. [28]

These temporal and spatial details play an important role in setting the tone for what follows. This is supported by the rest of what we find in the introductory section of the book.

The short programmatic speech of Yahweh in Deut. 1.6-8 sets up a paradigm for Israel's progress into the land—from Horeb straight to Canaan. This has the effect of giving the whole of chs. 1–3 the character of a diversion from the ideal, preparing the way for the necessity of the Anti-Exodus, and also the recapitulation of the experiences of Horeb and Kadesh Barnea.

Perhaps the most awkward passage of the narrative to deal with is the recollection at this point of the appointment of the judges (1.9-18). This section has usually been regarded as intrusive, with no relevance to the rest of the chapter. It shows close contact with the traditions of both Exodus 18 and Numbers 11 and has been ascribed to a redactional re-working of the traditions out of a desire to venerate Moses (by excluding Jethro and stressing the role of the people).[29] This does not seem to be the main concern of the text, nor does it account for its current position.

In view of the narrative that follows, and in particular the recasting of the tradition to emphasize the role of the people, it seems likely that the significance of these verses lies in their depiction of the devolution of political, judicial and spiritual authority which had occurred since the departure from Egypt.[30] The preceding verses have set the scene for

28. Targum Onqelos to Deut. 1.1. See B. Grossfeld, *Targum Onqelos to Deuteronomy* (Edinburgh: T. & T. Clark, 1988). For recent support see P.D. Miller, *Deuteronomy* (Interpretation; Louisville: John Knox Press, 1990), p. 22.

29. Von Rad, *Deuteronomy*, p. 38, and especially Mayes, *Deuteronomy*, pp. 119—'While in Exodus it is Moses himself who takes responsibility for choosing rulers for the people, here in Dt. 1.13ff. it is the people who themselves choose their commanders and consequently bear the responsibility for their choice. This is particularly relevant in the present overall context of the people's rebellion against the commandment of Yahweh to take possession of the land'; Noth, *Deuteronomistic History*, pp. 31, 51, struggles to make any sense of their inclusion, offering the explanation that they are to provide information regarding the command of the Israelite army in the battles of the conquest. This does violence to the text, and must be dismissed. See also Lohfink, 'Darstellungskunst', pp. 109-11.

30. I take Exod. 18.13-27 and Num. 11.16-25 to refer to separate incidents where administrative and 'spiritual' support was given to Moses. See G.J. Wenham, *Numbers* (TOTC; Leicester: IVP, 1981), p. 108. Thus there is no necessary contradiction

Israel's possession of Yahweh's gift of land—those which follow begin to explain what went wrong. The purpose of 1.9-18 is to lay the responsibility for what follows squarely at the feet of the people as a whole. Moses, while sharing in the responsibility for the action of the nation, cannot be blamed for what happened in the wilderness. The careful reworking and combination of earlier material is designed to shift the focus from Moses as charismatic leader to the people themselves, while at the same time developing the powerful motif of national disobedience prohibiting even Moses from entering the land. The conclusion to the unit in v. 18 underlines the responsibility for the leaders chosen from and by the community in all that follows.

In the 'spy-narrative' which follows, Kadesh Barnea is presented as the archetypal 'place of decision'. In vv. 19-25 the choice facing Israel is presented in a way that leaves no-one in doubt as to the preferable alternative—the desert is 'vast' and 'dreadful', but the land of Canaan is the land promised to the Patriarchs, which is pronounced 'good', possibly with overtones of Edenic abundance. The reticence of the people in vv. 26-28 arises from the size of the inhabitants and the size of their fortifications, and despite the divine cajoling in vv. 29-33, Israel decides to stay firmly put. It is interesting that in contrast to the Numbers account the reconnaissance is the initiative of the people, and their reticence depicted in the worst possible terms (v. 25).

In the next few verses, as the consequences of national disobedience are spelled out, the purpose of the inclusion of the Kadesh Barnea narrative in this historical retrospect becomes apparent. Disobedience leads to exclusion from the land. The decision which Israel made at Kadesh Barnea had drastic after-effects. The inclusion of this story here implies that the issues facing the nation in Moab were equally grave.

The appearance of Caleb in 1.36 has caused some comment, especially since Joshua is omitted at this point, in contrast to Numbers 32. While it is possible that this is merely an 'innocent' inclusion of one element of the Kadesh tradition, it seems much more likely that here Caleb is held out as the man who made the right decision, and thus an appropriate role model for this generation of Israel. The exception made for Caleb is in stark contrast to the irreversible inclusion of Moses in the fate of the

---

between the ascription of the judicial 'idea' to Jethro in Exod. 18, the initiative of Yahweh in Num. 11 and the roles of Moses and people here. The purpose of the passage is not to give a blow-by-blow account of events, but to make a theological observation from Israel's experience which is pertinent to the narrative to follow.

generation of which he was leader. The casting of Caleb in the role of the 'true Israelite' draws a parallel between the fate of the people and of their leader. Yahweh proclaims to the people, 'Not you, but Caleb!', and to Moses, 'Not you, but Joshua'. This reinforces the urgency of the decision facing the nation *en masse*.[31]

The final paragraph further underlines the irreversibility of the decision, despite a change of heart of the people—Israel can do nothing to redress the situation, no matter how hard it tries. Its progress is seen to be contingent upon making the correct decision at Kadesh Barnea. Once the wrong choice has been made, the direct route into the land becomes an impossible dream (see e.g. v. 40). There can be no doubt that the moment of decision for Israel has now passed—Kadesh is no longer the place of opportunity, but has become a dead end. Instead Yahweh instigates an Anti-Exodus. The chapter ends with the journey into the land stalled at Kadesh, and there is little prospect of advance.

This closing scene supports once more the view set out above. Chapter 1 deals almost exclusively with the archetypal place of failure in Israel's history, Kadesh Barnea. Verse 2 brings it to mind and the rest of the chapter follows Israel's movement to their fateful refusal to enter the land. In the light of an introduction that repeatedly stresses the importance of geographical and temporal location, it is hard to avoid the conclusion that the Deuteronomist intends his readers to see the connection instantly between Kadesh, and the new place of decision on a new day 38 years later. Chapters 2 and 3 describe the journey that was necessary to bring Israel back to the place where it all went wrong.

While the journey of Israel is initiated in Deut. 1.6-8 by Yahweh, it is in chs. 2 and 3 that it properly gets under way for the Deuteronomist. Now, at last, Israel begins to move forward with some success. The text is packed with the language of journey. To some degree this is an inevitable consequence of the subject material, but it is probable that the

---

31.    This is supported by the interpretation given above for the appointment of the judges—one of the purposes of Moses' address is to divert attention from the national leader to the individual. For Mayes, however, the Deuteronomist, drawing on the J source 'was constrained to refer to Caleb here, not only out of fidelity to his source, but also as background for later material in his history (Joshua 14)' (*Deuteronomy*, p. 132). This is essentially the position of Noth, who argues that 'Caleb's exceptional conduct is the crux of the whole story', *Deuteronomistic History*, p. 50 n. 5. This is clearly overstating the case. Noth's contention that the narrative is careless with historical detail because it is reproducing a well-known story in effect undermines his desire to read it as a background to Josh. 14.

proliferation of reminders that Israel 'set out' or ' turned back' is in itself a deliberate device of the author. The idea is developed that, in contrast to the static conclusion to ch. 1 and the 'static' beginning to ch. 2 (with the divinely ordained aimless wandering in the hills of Seir), Israel should always be on the move.

The purposeful motion begins again almost at once, as the journey of reversal becomes a remedial journey. The rest of the chapter, and in fact the whole historical introduction, is concerned with the journey back to the edge of the land—not this time to Kadesh but to Moab. It is not a simple repetition of earlier events, for Israel should have learned much from its experience of moving in the wrong direction.

There are significant discrepancies between this version of the Israelite itinerary and that given in Numbers 20–21.[32] In view of the careful selection and presentation of historical incident seen in Deuteronomy 1, it seems reasonable at least to allow the possibility of a theological explanation which does not need to resort to positing a variant tradition.

The emphases which we find in the Deuteronomist's account which do not appear in the parallel section in Numbers are the grant of a land of their own to the Edomites, Moabites and Ammonites, the accompanying proscription of military action against them, the almost tacit obedience of Israel, and once more the reference to the decision and consequences of Kadesh Barnea in vv. 14-15. This oddly intrusive break to the flow of the story, passed over by most commentators, may be the clue to understanding the writer's purpose in retelling events in this peculiar way.

Two distinct themes are intertwined here: the first is an ironic contrast of the Israelites' failure to occupy the land presented as such an appealing option at Kadesh Barnea, and the success of the other nations in taking possession of Yahweh's 'gift' to them! This is emphasized in the parentheses of vv. 10-12 and 20-23, as a rather sneering reminder of the other nations' success in wresting land from giants is taken up.[33] The

32.  This is set out in detail by e.g. Mayes, *Deuteronomy*, pp. 144-45.

33.  It is unnecessary to say that the writer is trying to blur the uniqueness of Israel's relationship with Yahweh, or of his unique gift to them, but is using irony to highlight the ludicrous situation national rebellion has led to. The argument almost amounts to 'qal wahomer'. There is a sense of Israel being a laughing stock, rather than evidently 'God's treasured possession', as we see in e.g. Ezek. 36.16. This is not a common biblical idea. The question of the parentheses in vv. 10-12 and 20-23 is not difficult—whether they are a part of the fabric of the original text or not, they are in complete sympathy with the tone and direction of the rest of the passage. This

second concern of the passage is with the purgative and educative power of the wilderness period. There is a tension between the affirmation of Yahweh's care, oversight and provision in the desert in v. 7 and the blunt reminder of the generation who perished during this time. This harsh juxtaposition could be a deliberate device of the author in harnessing the painful memories of the rejection of God's way at Kadesh and the subsequent experience in the wilderness to the knowledge of the beneficence of Yahweh, in an attempt to remind them of the dire consequences of disobedience once more.

It is difficult to dispute the existence of a carefully conceived ethical agenda underlying the construction of this 'historical' section—and therefore to follow Noth's conclusion that the details are included purely as background to a Deuteronomistic interpretation of history. The experience of the nations is spelled out not from any historiographical interest, but to provoke the Israelites to jealousy and expose to them the folly of their past actions, while impressing on them the reprieve they have been given in being brought back to their 'new Kadesh Barnea' in Moab. It seems to me that the difficulties in comparing the versions of the Wilderness wanderings in Deuteronomy 2 and Numbers 20–21 arise from the radically different purposes of the rehearsals of the events, rather than primarily any difference in the sources behind them.

As the instructions for the resumption of the journey towards the land are given, a parenthesis in Deut. 2.13-16 draws our attention to the fact that the time in the wilderness has removed the recalcitrant generation in its entirety from Israel. This is then followed by a further divine directive to continue the advance, now that this 'impediment' has been dealt with.

This whole section has shown that 'journey' material is carefully shaped by the author to highlight the significance of the failure of Israel at Kadesh, culminating in the death of the Wilderness generation, and thus to underline the potential of the 'second chance' at Moab. A secondary theme is that the people of God must always remain on the move. (This, as we shall see, obtains also in the law-code, contrary to the impression there of a movement towards an eventual settlement.)

The next stage in the narrative is the campaigns against Sihon and Og. Once more the dominant motif is that of moving on towards the land of promise (2.24, 3.1). Indeed the sole cause of conflict with Sihon (and by

poses severe problems for attempts to drive a wedge between the voice of Moses and that of the narrator. See also the refrain taken up in 9.2.

implication with Og) is the refusal of passage for the nation on the way to Canaan (vv. 27-29). It is in this context of continuing journey that the division of the Transjordan region is introduced. Clearly in the Deuteronomic scheme it is to be taken as a preliminary to the occupation of Canaan proper—a 'dry-run' for the armies of Israel, presenting both the possibility of success in battle and occupation.[34]

Moses' reluctant concession to those wishing to remain in Transjordan (after his denunciation of such a suggestion as a return to the equivocating of the previous 'Kadesh' generation) in Numbers 32 finds no echo here. The sense of foreboding for those remaining outside Canaan, as if they are starting on a course fraught with danger, is much less prominent. Rather the purpose of this selective account is to present the occupation of Transjordan as a prelude to the conquest proper and thus encourage the people to choose to obey Yahweh today in the light of the success that obedience had occasioned in the past.[35] His concerns are hortatory and ethical rather than merely historiographic. The Sihon and Og narratives are recounted to inform the action of Israel at Moab, in contrast to the failure of Kadesh Barnea.

This interpretation is given some support by its proximity to the following pericope, Deut. 3.21-28, which deals with the exclusion of Moses from the land due to the *disobedience of the people*. Every detail sharpens the focus on the necessity of Israel reversing the tragic decision of Kadesh.

The conclusion of this whole section leaves the reader in a state of uncertainty—Israel is left 'near Beth Peor'. Yet again we have a seemingly irrelevant geographical note.[36] In view of the recorded apostasy in Numbers, however, this surely is another use of 'place' to heighten the rhetorical effect of the book. As the memory of Kadesh Barnea and Horeb was deliberately evoked in 1.2, so here another place of national disaster, this time in the experience of all who listened, is recalled—Israel

---

34.    There is some conflict within the OT concerning the position of Transjordan in the land—see e.g. H.E. von Waldow, Israel and her Land: Some Theological Considerations', in *A Light unto my Path: Old Testament Studies in Honor of J.M. Myers* (ed. H. Bream; Philadelphia: Temple University Press, 1974), pp. 493-508, esp. 498, for a discussion of this.

35.    3.18-20 show that the Deuteronomist knew *at least* of a similar tradition to that of Numbers. His primary interest is to use the manner of the conquest of Transjordan as a paradigm for Israel.

36.    The occurrence in Josh. 13.20 is of no help. It is inconceivable that the Deuteronomy reference was intended as background for Joshua.

cannot repeat the mistakes of the past. Yahweh had graciously allowed them to reach this point, despite a record which was far from unblemished. Now they must take their chance, or the consequences will be disastrous.

*Conclusions*

I began by examining the work of Martin Noth on the Deuteronomistic character of the opening chapters of Deuteronomy. This raised several critical questions concerning the conventional interpretation of the text. The primary concern was the rigid dichotomy established between the content of these chapters and what is to follow. A rhetorical study of Deuteronomy 1–3 reveals that there are profound theological themes determining its structure and content which do not sit easily with a Deuteronomistic origin.

The prologue to the book presents two foundational concepts. The first is that Israel is a nation on the move—engaged on a journey with Yahweh. This journey began in Egypt, and is still in progress at Moab. It involves every member of the Mosaic community, and the community's faithfulness to the covenant of Yahweh is mirrored by its course. The second concept cannot be separated from the first, since it asserts that the past experience of Israel holds the key to enjoyment of their covenant relationship. If Israel is to enter the land and live at peace in it, then the lessons of the past must be absorbed into the national consciousness.

Deuteronomy opens with an account of the journey of Israel to date which inevitably imbues what follows with a dynamic element. The impression is carefully created that for Israel, a life of obedience is life on the move towards the land. Chapters 1–3 instigate a journey which is physical, theological and ethical. Yahweh has acted; Israel must respond by moving forward. But the development of the journey motif is only preliminary—it is not described in such detail in these chapters only to have it grind to a halt at Moab. At the end of ch. 3 we are left in suspense concerning precisely what is to come, but expecting the dynamic to continue.

On this journey, the categories of time and place converge. As I have already pointed out, the people of Israel standing at Moab are not simply *observers* of the journey, but are addressed as *participants* in it. The insistence that the past events related by the writer involved his hearers is relentless. God is said to have spoken to '*us*' at Horeb (1.7, 9), Moses addresses '*you*' (1.18), and every aspect of the ensuing journey, every decision, every battle involves every person in Moses' audience. These chapters breathe contemporaneity and inclusivity, demanding the attention of everyone listening. It seems that what we have here is not only salvation history, but an exposition of the *way* of salvation in the present and the future, based on the national experience of the past. The events of the past and the places of the past coalesce with those of the present, *so that Israel might walk in the ways of Yahweh*. This 'journey' means more to the Deuteronomist than a simple transition from the life of the wilderness to the paradisal agrarian existence set before them in Canaan. The 'journey' is a pregnant metaphor for life with Yahweh.

It was suggested that if theological connections could be established between Deuteronomy 1–3 and the rest of the book, then the case for separation of these chapters would be severely undermined. In demonstrating that chs. 1–3 are concerned above all else to set Israel on her way, *viz.* to establish 'journey' as a theological and ethical concept which embraces the past of Israel and makes demands upon its future, we have uncovered criteria which may be of use in showing such a theological integrity.[37] Chapter 4, which in many ways is the key to the use of 'time and place' in the book as a whole, evinces the development of this theological agenda introduced in chs. 1–3, as the metaphor of 'journey' and the significance of times and places in the life of Israel with Yahweh is unfolded.

## 2. *Time and Place in Chapter 4:*
### *The Identification of Moab with Horeb*

Chapter 4 is probably the most complex chapter in the whole book of Deuteronomy. It is laden with theological meaning, and yet critical problems have hindered every attempt to interpret the text.

### *History of Interpretation*
Two major problems have consistently dogged the interpretation of this chapter. The first is primarily literary—the chapter is studded with number changes, which occur with a frequency unparalleled in the rest

---

37.  Support for such a view comes from a surprising quarter: 'Es gibt hier kaum ein theologisches Motiv ohne Bezug zum Kern des Dtn' (L. Perlitt, 'Deuteronomium 1–3 im Streit der exegetischen Methoden', in *Das Deuteronomium* [ed. N. Lohfink; BETL, 68; Leuven: Leuven University Press, 1985], p. 158).

of the book. The other point of contention has a literary dimension, but is essentially theological—this is the relationship of ch. 4 to both the preeminently historical material which precedes it and the parenesis which it introduces.

While most commentators are ready to acknowledge the conceptual unity of the chapter, literary coherence is a different matter. This criterion, in fact, divides critics into two broad groups. On the one hand Steuernagel, von Rad, Noth and Knapp insist on the composite nature of the text, while Lohfink, Braulik, Mittmann and Mayes defend its unity.[38] The arguments run to many pages, often revolving around the nature of the *Numeruswechsel*. If one accepts that the change in number is a stylistic device then the obstacles to viewing the chapter as a single unit are significantly reduced.

The major changes of number in Deuteronomy 4 occur in vv. 3-4, 19-20, 21-22, 23-26, 34-35. The most thoroughgoing account of this phenomenon is given by Braulik in the closely argued and substantial *Die Mittel deuteronomischer Rhetorik erhoben aus Deuteronomium 4.1-40*.[39] Braulik's painstaking analysis leads him to the conclusion that change of number is not a suitable criterion for source or redactional criticism. He sees in the rough division of the chapter into plural (1-28) and singular (29-40) an overarching attempt to confirm that the promise of Yahweh still stands for the exilic generations. Despite losing the land, and thus being deprived of the opportunity to obey the letter of the (Deuteronomic) law, Israel can still have a meaningful relationship with Yahweh, characterized by grace and obedient response. Within these sections the central concerns are marked by a switch from plural–singular–plural (3-4, 10-11, 19-20, 21-22) or singular–plural–singular (34-35).[40] The multiple changes in 23-26 (v. 23: plural–singular; 25:

38. See D. Knapp, *Deuteronomium 4: Literarische Analyse und theologische Interpretation* (Göttingen: Vandenhoeck & Ruprecht, 1987) for an analysis of recent work. Knapp's main arguments will be considered by McConville in this volume.

39. (AnBib, 68; Rome: Pontifical Biblical Institute, 1978). See also 'Weisheit, Gottesnähe und Gesetz—Zum Kerygma von Deuteronomium 4,5-8', in *Studien zum Pentateuch* (FS W. Kornfeld; ed. G. Braulik; Vienna: Herder & Herder, 1977), pp. 165-95, reprinted in *Studien zur Theologie des Deuteronomiums* (Stuttgarter Biblische Aufsatzbände, Altes Testament, 2; Stuttgart: Katholisches Bibelwerk, 1988), pp. 53-93. This paper is discussed in some detail below.

40. 'Die häufigste Funktion des Numeruswechsels ist das *Herausheben von Höhepunkten innerhalb einzelner Abschnitte*, deren Struktur damit schärfer profiliert wird' (Braulik, *Die Mittel*, p. 149).

singular–plural–singular; 26: singular–plural) serve to heighten the stress
on the final warning against idolatry. This treatment of Braulik's has
never been adequately refuted.

Alongside the work of Braulik, Lohfink also understands the text as
an exilic attempt to address the question of obeying the law in Babylon.
Chapter 4 then functions as a hermeneutical key for the rest of the book
in its final Deuteronomistic form.[41] A fresh interpretation of the Horeb
theophany enables a redefinition of Yahweh's covenant demands in
terms of exclusive worship in a pluralistic environment, preaching the
*Hauptgebot* to the exile. This is set against the background of separation
from and the destruction of Solomon's temple.

Braulik, backing up the stylistic observations of *Die Mittel deuteronomischer* Rhetorik with a theological rationale for the shape and contents
of the chapter in 'Weisheit, Gottesnähe und Gesetz', argues that the
decisive element in the chapter is to be found in vv. 5-8. Here, echoing
the Deuteronomistic concepts introduced in the prayer of Solomon in
1 Kings 8 at the dedication of the temple, a concerted effort is made to
enable a new appropriation of the Horeb revelation. Obedience to the
law is now defined in terms of a new Solomonic wisdom. It is through
this *religiös ethische Haltung* that the promises to the Patriarchs may
still be realized. This new concept of wisdom is coupled to a 'relocation'
of the presence of God in heaven—a reaffirmation of the transcendence
of Yahweh which enables his presence to remain a reality in the life of
the people in the wake of deportation and the razing of the temple.

These are both helpful and stimulating studies. Clearly, for example,
the wisdom language of Deut. 4.5-8, and the unusual formulation of the
supremacy of Israel, are striking and require an explanation. It is not certain, however, that these verses should be read in the light of Solomon's
prayer. The assertion that Yahweh is close to Israel when they pray
is too vague to be identified as an extension of 1 Kgs 8.27-32. In fact
there is a remarkable degree of common ground—Solomon appears to
be affirming that answered prayer depends on the transcendence of

---

41. In addition to the works already cited see Lohfink, 'Verkündigung des
Hauptgebots in der jüngsten Schicht des Deuteronomiums', originally in *BibLeb* 5
(1964), and in a modified form as 'Höre, Israel! Auslegung von Texten aus dem Buch
Deuteronomium', *Die Welt der Bibel* 18 (Düsseldorf, 1965), reprinted in *Studien zum
Deuteronomium und zur Deuteronomischen Literatur*, I (Stuttgarter Biblische
Aufsatzbände, Altes Testament, 8; Stuttgart: Katholisches Bibelwerk, 1990), pp. 167-
92. Also Braulik, 'Weisheit', pp. 55-56.

Yahweh more than on the confines of his temple! It seems that the progression from Deuteronomy 4 to 1 Kings 8 is one from the general to the particular, rather than *vice versa*. The meaning of 'wisdom' here is puzzling, and too general to be of any use in fixing the provenance of the unit. All that can be said is that 'wisdom' is used to affirm that even in the eyes of the nations the way of Yahweh is indisputably best. Such a sentiment could have easily been expressed at almost any stage in Israel's history. Nor does it make any statement concerning the existence or non-existence of the Jerusalem temple.This leads us to a third dubious assumption of Braulik and Lohfink—that the concept of Yahweh's presence necessarily implies a response to the annihilation of the temple. Such dogmatism fails to take account of the Deuteronomic context. In the early chapters of Deuteronomy the concept of the presence of Yahweh is most readily associated with the Exodus/ Wilderness traditions. It is most likely that the primary reference in ch. 4 is to this idea of 'presence', in contrast to the capricious Canaanite deities tied to their sanctuaries, rather than a firmly developed temple ideology.[42]

I would suggest that the groundwork done in the previous section, uncovering the importance of the journey of Israel in Deuteronomy, is vital in the interpretation of ch. 4. Now ideas of time and place are unfolded. A new parallel is drawn between the events of Horeb (and in particular the theophany) and the moment of national decision at Moab, in the broader context of polemic against Canaanite polytheism. In addition to this the journey motif is extended far into the future, as the corporate experience and responsibility of Israel is explored in depth. Chapter 4, then, cannot be simply characterized as a late reinterpretation of the history of the nation, nor even a reappropriation of earlier insights for the crisis of Babylon. It is an integral part of the rhetoric of Deuteronomy.

### Horeb and the Parenesis of Deuteronomy 4

This chapter both assumes and develops the concepts of place and time underlying the journey theme which was shown to be at the centre of chs. 1–3. The centre of gravity of chs. 1–3 was the identification of Moab with Kadesh Barnea. That equation having been established, the focus now shifts to Horeb.

A concerted attempt is made in Deuteronomy 4 to link both the

---

42. For the idea of presence in relation to 'name-theology', see further McConville, below.

*content* of the revelation at Horeb and the *manner* of the revelation to the experience of Israel at Moab, in order to make theological and ethical points. The major concerns are to relate the theophany at Horeb to the Mosaic preaching of 'law' at Moab, and to introduce the key Deuteronomic tension between the transcendence and immanence of Yahweh. The latter will be discussed in some detail by McConville. In addition to this we are provided with an overview of the grand perspectives of the book, as the past, present and future are juxtaposed, creating the hinge on which the whole book is suspended.

The rhetoric of Deuteronomy 4 sets it apart both from the preceding material and all that follows. To begin with there is a very obvious change of style and tone in 4.1.[43] The sustained retrospect of chs. 1–3 is now replaced by direct address to Moses' contemporaries, changing the focus from the fact of the imminent ethical crisis to the precise response required by Yahweh. Polzin points out that this is reflected in a change of narrative technique :

> Chapter 4 stands off from the first three chapters not only by its references to future rather than past events and utterances, but also by the fact that its reported speech is predominantly in indirect discourse, whereas the reported speech in chs. 1–3 was overwhelmingly in direct discourse.[44]

The chapter begins very firmly rooted in the present, introducing one expression which plays a crucial role in understanding the purpose not only of this chapter, but of the rest of the book. In particular, the scope and meaning of החקים והמשפטים has profound implications for the place of the Decalogue and its relationship to the Deuteronomic law.

The stereotyped formula החקים והמשפטים occurs in 4.1, 5, 8, 14, 45; 5.1, 31; 6.1, 20; 7.11; 11.31; 12.1 and 26.16, 17. It has been the subject of much discussion.[45] The importance of the phrase is compounded by the fact that, in addition to introducing ch. 4, it appears to frame *both* the parenesis of chs. 5–11 *and* the lawcode of chs. 12–26. The phrase has

---

43.　Cf. the emphatic uses in 10.25 and 26.10.

44.　*Moses and the Deuteronomist* (New York: Seabury, 1980), p. 40. Also Weinfeld, *Deuteronomy*: 'Unlike Deut. 1–3, which uses past events and historical facts in order to educate the people, this chapter uses, for the same purpose, religious ideology on the one hand and rhetorical media on the other' (p. 214).

45.　Most notably by G. Braulik, 'Die Ausdrücke für "Gesetz" im Buch Deuteronomium', *Bib* 51 (1970), pp. 40-66, and Lohfink, 'Die "*huqqim umispatim*" im Buch Deuteronomium und ihre Neubegrenzung durch Dtn. 12.1', *Bib* 70 (1989), pp. 1-27.

little intrinsic meaning of any significance. Outside Deuteronomy its occurrences are general and varied. Within the book, however, it is used in a considered and meaningful way to make a pivotal theological point. Chapter 4 cannot be understood without appreciating the significance of this Deuteronomic coinage.

One puzzling feature of the occurrences of this phrase in Deuteronomy 4 is that despite being heralded with a flourish in 4.1, there is nothing in the chapter which warrants such a description. In fact they do not seem to arrive for some considerable time! This has prompted much speculation.

The most detailed work on this word-pair has been done once more by Lohfink and Braulik. In the section in his article 'Die Ausdrücke für "Gesetz"' on החקים והמשפטים in the book as a whole, Braulik argues that, while used with various nuances, it basically denotes the whole of the Mosaic preaching, covering chs. 5–26. This is in keeping with his overall conclusion that there is no word or phrase in Deuteronomy which refers to the lawcode in isolation. The החקים והמשפטים are definitely not the stipulations given by Moses in contrast to those revealed by Yahweh at Horeb. Rather the *Doppelausdruck* is to be taken in a more general way, like 'torah'.[46] Braulik also resists any attempt to show that the meaning of the phrase shifts as the book develops. In particular he takes Merendino to task for his contention that in Deut. 5.1 the phrase denotes the Decalogue, while in 5.31 it has become the corpus of chs. 12–26.[47]

The force of Braulik's paper is considerable—he carefully shows for ten 'legal' expressions that they never mean the laws of chs. 12–26 alone, but always encompass the whole teaching of the book. His conclusion is that the phrase החקים והמשפטים is used in such a way as to unite the Decalogue, the Mosaic preaching and the Lawcode under a single rubric.

Lohfink's method and findings are significantly different. His argument is founded on the belief that the key to unlocking the Deuteronomic use of החקים והמשפטים is to be found in the appositional phrase in 1 Sam. 30.25, where משפט qualifies חק. This lies behind Deut. 5.31 and 6.1, where a tripartite phrase occurs (המצוה והחקים והמשפטים). The use in 1 Samuel provided a pre-exilic compiler a means of qualifying 'the commandment' in such a way as to facilitate the integration

---

46. 'Die "*huqqim umispatim*"', p. 62 .
47. R.P. Merendino, *Das Deuteronomische Gesetz* (BBB, 31; Bonn: Peter Hanstein , 1969), p. 13 n. 9.

of the arcane and archaic stipulations of chs. 12–26 into the rest of the
book.[48] The new phrase החקים והמשפטים not only provided the author
with a way of explaining what the 'commandment' was, but enabled
him to develop his whole view of the law along specific lines, linking
obedience to the Lawcode firmly to occupation of the land. This
involved binding the Decalogue to the Deuteronomic Law, and his
exhortation (broadly chs. 6–11) to both. Much of this was achieved by
supplying ch. 5, providing an aetiology of החקים והמשפטים and a
grounding for all that follows.[49] This inspired the much later reflections
of ch. 4. This construction seems based on a rather shaky identification
of 5.31 and 6.1 as the earliest Deuteronomic uses by analogy with
1 Samuel, and ultimately sheds little light on Deuteronomy 4.

There is agreement that the use of the phrase החקים והמשפטים has some
role to play in the development of the Deuteronomic understanding of
'law'. Beyond this insight, there has been little agreement. I believe,
however, that the idea of the journey of Israel through time and place,
stopping at places of significance for covenant faithfulness presented in
chs. 1–3 provides the solution to the Deuteronomist's ingenious use of
this formula.

We have already noted that, after the introductory chapters have
selectively recounted the journey of Israel to Moab, with the emphasis
on the new opportunity for Israel to decide for Yahweh, ch. 4 begins
with a reference to החקים והמשפטים. The phrase is so prominent in the
chapter that it is probable that the chapter's intention is, in some degree
at least, to introduce the idea of החקים והמשפטים. In the rhetorical
development of the book, we have reached a point where we would
expect some statement of the content of the decision facing Israel in the
present. This is exactly what we get in this phrase.

The first reference to החקים והמשפטים in 4.1 announces that the
response demanded of Israel *is* well-defined, and will be defined as we
proceed. Thus there seems to be an anticipatory vagueness about the
phrase here, raising the question 'what are these laws and statutes?'.
This is precisely the question which ch. 4, and indeed the whole of
Deuteronomy, seeks to answer. Neither Lohfink nor Braulik allows for a
sufficient degree of subtlety here. In one sense it refers, as Braulik insists,
to the whole of Deuteronomy 5–26, which we could call the revelation

---

48. 'Die "*huqqim umispatim*"', p. 9. Lohfink's conclusions are considered in a
slightly different context by McConville (see below).
49. Lohfink, 'Die "*huqqim umispatim*"', p. 7.

at Moab (although I would not want to exclude chs. 4 and 27–30 from this). In another sense the epithet demands a more immediate and concrete reference—this is found in the first instance in the content of the revelation at Horeb in ch. 5.

This ambiguity dominates ch. 4. In 4.5, there is little doubt that the reference is to the revelation at Moab. The use of ראה is important in that it forms a link between the recent experience of the consequences of apostasy at Baal-Peor and the call to heed the והמשפטים חקים. It also implies that this corpus is to be heard by the same generation who experienced Baal-Peor (that is, not the Horeb generation—although the identification of the hearers with their predecessors is to be essential to the rhetoric of the chapter, as we shall see; cf. vv. 10, 15). ראה occurs in a similar context, urging a decision to go forward into the land with Yahweh, in 1.8, 11.26, 30.15 and possibly 32.49.[50] The verb למדתי may be an example of a 'declarative perfect', or perhaps better an 'instantaneous perfective which represents a situation occurring at the very instant the expression is being uttered', often used with *verba dicendi*.[51] The force of 4.5 would then be to present החקים והמשפטים to the Israelites as the utterances of Moses now in progress ('I hereby teach you'). There is substantial continuity with the lessons of chs. 1–3.

In keeping with the Deuteronomist's concern for the reputation of Yahweh and Israel among the nations, the intention of 4.8 is to show that these חקים ומשפטים are the archetype of justice.[52] In doing this, the 'laws and statutes' are equated with this 'torah'. Here, as in 1.5, it seems that 'torah' is being used to denote the whole of the preaching that follows. Thus in 4.8 the general prospect of 4.5 is maintained. החקים והמשפטים is used to point to the identifiable core of what is to come, which could be expressed in terms of the demand to respond to Yahweh in line with the Mosaic declaration of his will. It is still unclear where precisely such guidance is to be found.

In v. 14 the picture begins to become clearer—the declaration of החקים והמשפטים is traced back to the theophany at Horeb. Moses' role of

50. It is also a prominent feature of the journey narrative of chs. 1–3—cf. 1.21, 2.24, 31, 3.27. Deut. 4.5 (and 4.3) binds chap. 4 to this introductory section.

51. See GKC §106i. (also Mayes, p. 150, Noth, *et al.*) and B.K. Waltke and M. O'Connor, *Biblical Hebrew Syntax* (Winona Lake, IN: Eisenbrauns, 1990), p. 488, respectively.

52. This is discussed in my forthcoming thesis, *The Ethics of Deuteronomy* (DPhil dissertation; Oxford University, 1994).

teaching (cf. 4.1) is the subject of a specific divine instruction. Although both the content and the ultimate origin of the material remains tantalizingly ambiguous, we can be certain that the writer is forging a link between what happened at Horeb, and the events in progress at Moab. The phrase בעת ההוא has the subtle effect of drawing attention to the similarities between the two places of revelation by pointing out their differences.

The rest of ch. 4, as we shall see in a moment, is essentially a meditation on the events of Horeb. The central concern is to set before Israel the revelation of God there and the response demanded of Israel, which is summed up in 4.40. It is interesting that here, where one might expect the stereotyped phrase to occur, it does not. Instead we have a synonymous expression. The author seems to have established that the decision can be described as obeying the laws and statutes, and does not feel bound to this wording. He reserves it for making *specific* points. This looseness in the use of law-language is illustrated by 4.44-45, where Torah is equated with not just החקים והמשפטים but also העדת. [53]

The repetition (and expansion) of the terms for the Mosaic stipulations/exhortation is crucial for understanding this chapter. There is little or nothing that could meet the description of החקים והמשפטים between 4.1 and 4.45. Why are they there? The answer seems to be that Deuteronomy 4 is developing the Deuteronomic concept of law, in a way which provides a smooth transition to ch. 5 and beyond. The introduction of and reflection on Horeb lays the foundations of a dynamic view of the law of God. On this view divine revelation is not merely about the transmission of a list of prescriptions, but deals with motivation also. The law includes the motivation to obey. This applies whether law is expressed as Torah, statute or commandment. Chapter 4 initiates the process by which the reader may see what החקים והמשפטים is all about. The rhetoric of Deuteronomy gathers pace and size like a snowball—by the end of ch. 4 we do not see the finished product, but

53.   This has caused a few problems for commentators. Lohfink argues that this is an old formulation which has been updated by a very late hand preoccupied with the language of החקים והמשפטים; 'Die "*huqqim umispatim*"', p. 11. The question which then must be answered is why the old formula has not been replaced. The term may have a covenantal background, and/or links with the Decalogue, which leads Mayes to think that it is העדת which is the late addition! It would be attractive to see a link between the Decalogue and the Deuteronomic preaching at this point. This coheres well with the following material, but does not have sufficient support in the text to be compelling.

by a process of repetition and gradual accretion we can see the nature of the law, the response of Israel growing larger and taking shape before us.

After the prohibition of tampering with the content of the declaration of Moab in 4.2, Moses returns immediately to the theme of place (cf. 12.32). This time the reference is not to Beth-Peor (3.29) but to Baal-Peor. This name occurs only here and in Hos. 9.10.[54] It seems likely that this is a deliberate alteration by the Deuteronomist to invest Peor with paradigmatic significance as an archetypal place of apostasy. The location of the nation in 3.29 places the whole discourse under a shadow of recent rebellion. The renaming of the place in 4.3 drives home to the Israelites that even at Moab, which is defined as a place of revelation in 4.1, they are in danger of rejecting Yahweh. Moab is the new Kadesh: Israel cannot afford to let it become the new Baal-Peor. It is impossible to separate the flow of thought which ends ch. 3 from that with which ch. 4 opens.

It is in this context of anti-Canaanite polemic that 4.5-8 is to be understood. The revelation at Moab is presented as preserving the national distinctiveness and showing the nations the superiority of life with Yahweh. The emphasis on the closeness of Yahweh to Israel at *all times* and in *all places* implies an inherent superiority over Canaanite gods like Baal of Peor. This transcendent dimension finds its immanent parallel in v. 8, where the laws and statutes are held up as concrete evidence of Yahweh's presence in Israel.[55] I have already argued that attempts to assert the transcendence of Yahweh in the wake of the demise of the immanence displayed by temple theology are unwarranted.[56]

*Time in Deuteronomy 4*

In Deuteronomy 1–4, the use of time has been relatively simple, drawing lessons for the present from past events. The use of 'today' at the end of 4.8 marks the beginning of a subtle and powerful new dimension to the

54.   See also Ps. 106.28, which provides indirect support for the position set out above.

55.   Since the ark is the resting place for the tablets of the law in Deuteronomy, it appears that the ark was still conceived of as demonstrating the real presence of Yahweh with his people. This throws into question attempts to see a concern to 'desacralise' the ark in the book.

56.   It is also betrays a basic misunderstanding of the Deuteronomist's concern to explore the tension between the transcendence and immanence of Yahweh. See McConville in this volume, and Millar, *Ethics*.

preaching of Moses. Initially 4.9 calls those listening to Moses' discourse to remember 'the things that you have seen with your own eyes'. In view of the recent demise of the Kadesh generation, and in context in ch. 4 this refers most naturally to the events at Baal-Peor. However in v. 10 Israel is called to 'Remember the day you stood before Yahweh your God at Horeb'. The glaring problem is that if we take 1.35 and 2.14 seriously, none of them *did* experience the Horeb theophany. Here Moses is employing a rhetorical technique involving the conflation of generations. The author intended his readers to see beyond the anachronism to the theological point behind it.[57]

It seems then that Moses is calling Israel to *an act of corporate, imaginative remembrance* as the insights of the past are brought to bear on the decisions of the present and future.[58] In doing so he binds the events of 'that day' (v. 10) to the unfolding events of Israel's 'today' at Moab. This draws attention to one of the most prominent temporal features of the book in Deuteronomy—the emphasis on 'today'.

It seems to have been von Rad who first highlighted the significance of the recurrence of היום for the interpretation of the book. Despite his perceptive observations on the motif, the full implications of his work have never been fully explored:

> It is the common denominator of the Deuteronomic homiletic as a whole...It cannot be maintained that this is merely an effective stylistic device which the Deuteronomist has chosen to make more vivid what he has to say. On the contrary, it is a quite fundamental feature of Deuteronomy...[59]

He helpfully speaks of the 'emphatic contemporaneity' which saturates Deuteronomy, arising in part from the prolific use of היום.[60] Sixty-two

---

57.   In any case it is reasonable to assume that a significant number of the Israelites would have died *anyway*, even if the death of the Kadesh generation is denied. The point still remains that for the Israel of today the events of Moab are to be equated with the long past national experience at Horeb.

58.   The terminology here, if not the actual formulation of the ideas, is close to that of Walter Brueggemann. See especially 'Imagination as a Mode of Fidelity', in *Understanding the Word: Essays in Honour of B.W. Anderson* (ed. J.T. Butler, E.W. Conrad and B.C. Ollenburger; JSOTSup, 37; Sheffield; JSOT Press, 1985), pp. 1-27.

59.   Von Rad, *The Problem of the Hexateuch and other Essays* (ET; London: Oliver & Boyd, 1966), p. 26.

60.   Von Rad, *The Problem of the Hexateuch*, p. 29.

times 'today' is used to focus on the decision facing Israel at Moab, and to heighten the urgency of making the right response.[61] In addition to this there are five examples in the historical retrospect which may well be a deliberate introduction to the 'catchword' (1.39; 2.18, 22, 25, 30), seven possible allusions in material dealing with Horeb 1.10; 4.10, 15; 5.24; 9.10; 10.4; 18.16), six associated with future life in Canaan (6.24; 26.3; 27.2; 31.17, 18) and two associated with the death of Moses which may echo the ideas of the earlier parts of the book (31.2; 32.48).

Whether we are moving in the atmosphere of Kadesh in ch. 2, or Horeb in chs. 4 and 5, the place of entry, or occupation or even return in ch. 30, there is a consistent concern to draw attention to the decision facing Israel היום, 'today'. While the main focus is the present decision at Moab, the author has used the notion of היום throughout the book to harness the past, present and future in all manner of places to the decision faced by Israel today at Moab.

DeVries has examined the biblical concept of the 'day' at some length. He agrees that the concept of the 'day' often transcends a wooden and literal understanding:

> As we analyse the use of the present *yôm*, we soon see that a basic distinction needs to be made between the day that is historically present in existential distinctiveness and the day that is present in gnomic discourse or in cultic regulation. The latter refers to a 'today' that is continually repeated and hence continuously present.[62]

He helpfully divides the occurrences with past, present and future reference, characterizing the 'day past as a moment of revelatory confrontation' and the day future 'as a new opportunity for decisive action'.[63] The present use, 'today', is much more varied, but in the context of our study a use to denote a day of decision for Israel is clearly apposite. All three of these temporal perspectives appear in ch. 4 as the importance of the response of Israel to Yahweh's ongoing revelation is informed by the

---

61. 4.4, 8, 20, 26, 38, 39, 40; 5.1, 3; 6.6; 7.11; 8.1, 11, 18, 19; 9.1, 3, 6; 10.13, 15; 11.2, 4, 8, 13, 26, 27, 28, 32; 12.8; 13.19; 15.5, 15; 19.9; 26.16, 17, 18; 27.1, 4, 9, 10, 11; 28.1, 13, 14, 15; 29.3, 9, 11, 12, 15, 17, 27; 30.2, 8, 11, 15, 16, 18, 19; 31.21; 32.46.

62. S.J. deVries, *Yesterday, Today and Tomorrow: Time and History in the Old Testament* (London: Eerdmans, 1975), p. 45.

63. S.J. deVries, *Yesterday, Today and Tomorrow*, pp. 126, 136, 323—'a summarising characterisation concerning a particular day in which Israel's God was in some way seen to be in crucial confrontation with his people'.

past, particularly at Horeb, and shown to be crucial to their future in the
land and beyond.

I have suggested that Deuteronomy builds on the concept of Israel's
ethical journey. This journey begins in Egypt, passes through Kadesh
and the Wilderness to Moab, and then on to Canaan to face the future.
Every stage of the journey can be comprehended and successfully
negotiated at Moab the place of decision. That picture can now be
augmented by adding that the journey of Israel must consist of a series
of 'todays'—the future of Israel is encapsulated in 'today at Moab'.
Each stage of national life—crossing the Jordan, pausing at Shechem
and stretching on into the far reaches of Israel's experience in the land
and out of it—can only be negotiated by responding in the same way as
'today at Moab'. In ch. 4 it is made plain that Israel must take on board
and respond to the revelation at Moab in exactly the same way as that
received at Horeb.

The rest of the account of the Horeb theophany in vv. 11-14 stresses
the presence of the assembled nation to such a degree that it is very
difficult to avoid detecting a deliberate rhetorical identification of the
events at Horeb and the impending preaching of law at Moab. There is
no difference in the 'you' who stood at Horeb, and the 'you' who are
now on the verge of the land, awaiting the further exposition of the law.
The retrospective focus of the opening chapters of the book consistently
aims to confront the present generation with the binding reality of the
events of the past. This method aims to draw the whole experience of
Israel from Egypt to Horeb to Moab (via the diversions of Kadesh) into
the environment of the ethical decisions facing every individual. The
ethical history of a nation coalesces into the series of 'ethical moments'
which constitute the life of the individual. Each Israelite in effect was
present every step of the way from Egypt, and each decision should be
informed by the richness of his or her tradition.

The contents of the Horeb revelation are identified with the
Deuteronomic preaching but this is not the only significant element of
the tradition drawn upon by the author. In vv. 11-20 Moses expounds
the consequences of the mode of the Horeb revelation for the audience
at Moab. Verse 11 introduces the double motif of the fire and the cloud,
once again highlighting the Deuteronomic concern with transcendence
and immanence.[64] This tension arises in the same anti-Canaanite context

---

64.  Miller has perceptively observed: 'The Hebrew simply juxtaposes in stark
fashion as if to state a vivid paradox that cannot be explained: on the one hand, bright

as 4.6-8. Yahweh is the God who is accessible but not confined, who communicates but cannot be comprehended. Israel is to think back to Horeb, and respond in obedience to the divine word.

It is worth pausing for a moment to note how this is supported by the recurrent phrase בעת ההוא. Thirteen of the fifteen occurrences (which are restricted to the first ten chapters) are concerned with the communication of the divine command in the past, and the results of obedience to that command.[65] In ch. 1 the phrase occurs three times in the context of the establishment of the 'judiciary' (vv. 9, 16, 18). Here בעת ההוא serves to underline the national polity of the former generations—a problem arose and was addressed by Moses, with the solution, as v. 18 implies, being accepted without question by the people. In the rehearsal of events on the remedial journey of Israel, it is clear that in the days after Kadesh Barnea, Israel moved at the Lord's bidding and enjoyed unbroken success as a result. In 2.34, 3.4, 8 and 12 the campaign advances because of the obedience of those involved. Deut. 3.18 and 21 advance this slightly by reminding Israel of commands given in the past (to the nation and Joshua) which have yet to be carried out. The other examples come in the extended hortatory section of chs. 5–11, and once more are solely concerned with emphasizing the revelation of the divine command and the obedient response demanded of Israel.[66]

It seems conclusive that in 4.14, as elsewhere, the obedience of the past is described in order to summon Israel to obedience in the present. There is clearly a link between בעת ההוא in the past and the present day, in perfect keeping with what we have already observed concerning the careful identification of Moab with Horeb, and indeed the whole pre-history of Israel.

---

burning fire; on the other hand, the thickest black darkness. Thus are held together, as one, hiddenness and revelation, mystery and accessibility, transcendence and immanence' (*Deuteronomy*, p. 59). See McConville on this theme.

65. See the appendix in Plöger, *Untersuchungen*. His treatment is, however, very inconclusive. The exceptions are 3.23 and 9.20, which deal with Moses' pleading for a lifting of the prohibition on his entering the land, and interceding for Aaron in the wake of the Golden Calf incident. It could actually be argued that both of these *do* in fact cohere with the theme of obedience in the past enjoining obedience in the present, functioning as a strong warning to the people to learn from the mistakes of their leaders.

66. See 5.5 (on the 10 words), 10.1 (the second set of tablets) and 10.8 (the setting apart of the Levites).

Chapter 4 continues to develop the close association of Horeb with Moab in the most visual terms in v. 15. Here it is clear that the language is rhetorical rather than concrete. The implicit anti-Canaanite polemic of vv. 11-14 is now spelled out. The climax of this part of the argument comes in v. 20—because of Israel's election by Yahweh to be the people of his inheritance, demonstrated in the Exodus, their worship in general (and their decision at Moab in particular) is to be determined by the Horeb theophany. This note of election has close contact with chs. 7, 9 and 10.

At this point the text switches back to an idea familiar from Deuteronomy 1-3: the disqualification of Moses. We saw there the power of the introduction of the leader's exclusion from the land in order to urge the people not to repeat the sins of the past. Here the author uses the same image in the same way to expose the danger of the particular sin of idolatry. This reveals a similarity in the parenetic techniques of Deuteronomy 1-3 and 4 which is often not noticed. The assertion that Yahweh made a covenant with the Moab generation in some way through their antecedents at Horeb in v. 23 is also important (cf. ch. 29).

Thus far it is the impact of *memory* in the present ethical experience of Israel which has dominated the discussion.[67] At 4.25, however, we reach a major point of transition in the thought of the book. The implications for the future of the idea of remembering, while inevitably implicit to some degree, have been largely ignored. Now a crucial shift takes place which deals with specific possibilities in the future of Israel. As this future perspective is introduced, it becomes clear that Moab is not merely to be the summation of experience, but the point at which Israel is to live in the future, continually remembering the mighty acts of God and responding to him in obedience. Moab is not merely the gateway to the land, but encapsulates the ongoing precondition of existence in the land—to forget the lessons of history recapitulated at this crucial moment will lead to disaster (v. 26). Once more it is the failure to reject

---

67. See E.P. Blair, 'An Appeal to Remembrance: The Memory Motif in Deuteronomy', *Int* 15 (1961), pp. 41-47; Brueggemann, 'Memory and Imagination', and also *The Land* (OBT; Philadelphia: Fortress Press, 1977). Blair points out that 'In the Bible, memory is rarely simply psychological recall. If one remembers in the biblical sense, the past is brought into the present with compelling power. Action in the present is conditioned by what is remembered' (p. 43).

Canaanite ways completely which results in such a disaster.[68] In the vicious circle of events described, such apostasy can only result in Israel falling deeper into the same behaviour which caused its downfall in the first place (vv. 28-29). The Moab moment is not one to be passed through and then left behind—it contains the future possibilities of Israel. It is made clear in v. 27, after the admission of the possibility of Israel being expelled from the land, that the way of repentance and return leads inexorably back to Moab, and to Horeb beyond that. Only if this 'journey of repentance' is undertaken is return possible.[69]

Moab is presented as the place where the past and future of Israel coalesce in a single moment, the place where the decision to follow Yahweh must be reaffirmed in every generation. The remainder of the chapter serves only to underline this.

In vv. 32-34 we have a sweeping recapitulation not only of the history of Israel but of the whole cosmos—these 'former days' must determine the action of Israel in the present and future—leading to the climax of the section. Yet it is made clear that the events of the Exodus, culminating at Horeb, far outstrip all else. Knowledge of this history is the only way to confession of the nature of Yahweh, and this history is recounted to elicit a response (v. 35).

After Israel is called to a final response in the light of the transcendence and immanence of Yahweh (vv. 36-40), the list of the East Bank Cities of Refuge in 41-43 (in the third person) is most unexpected. However, while seeming to break sharply from the sustained argument of the rest of ch. 4, the inclusion of the Cities of Refuge at this point could conceivably be a carefully positioned reminder of the partial fulfilment of the promise which Israel has already seen. The East Bank experience is presented as a 'dry-run' reassuring the nation (particularly in view of the promise of v. 40) of the outcome of conquest of the land itself. This is a deliberate echo of ch. 3, as a reminder to the nation that Yahweh is fulfilling his promises, even in the granting the 'optional extra' of the East Bank.

This accords well with the summary of what has gone before in Deut. 4.44-49.[70] Much of the significant material in the opening three

---

68. It is remarkable that the normal word for 'exile' is omitted here.

69. Lohfink in 'Die Verkündigung', p. 186, comments on 4.30: 'Dann wird es wieder wie einst am Horeb auf Jahwes Stimme hören'.

70. Once more we see that what has been often regarded as the beginning of 'Urdt' would have been meaningless if not preceded by chs. 1–4. The selective

chapters is gathered together. The recapitulation of the dispossession of Sihon and Og, and the extent of the land, speak of the possibilities before Israel. Yet the juxtaposition of the land of Sihon with Beth-Peor maintains tension by reintroducing the possibility of apostasy. Once again, as we have noted, the formula 'these are the commands and statutes...' recurs. This continues to move Israel on towards the decision, even if the precise content of it still tantalizingly withheld.

*Conclusions*

This chapter displays both a significant amount of theological innovation and continuity with what has gone before. One of the main concerns is to demonstrate the inseparability of the preaching of Deuteronomy, including parenesis and lawcode, from the revelation at Horeb. At a formal level this is achieved in part by a careful use of the phrase החקים והמשפטים.

The pointed application of the history of Israel which dominates the opening chapters does not disappear in ch. 4—the setting at Baal-Peor, the preoccupation with the events of Horeb, the use of the disqualification of Moses, the cities of refuge and the allusions to Sihon and Og amply demonstrate the continuity—but there is a subtle advance in thinking. In ch. 4 (see especially 4.10, 15) the people at Moab are addressed as those who were present at Horeb. There is a corporate view of the nation which transcends temporal limitations. In chs. 1–3 the past is used to provide simple models of disobedience (Kadesh) and obedience (Transjordan). Israel must look back and take note. A new dimension dominates Deuteronomy 4, however. Former experiences of the nation are not merely historical examples, connected to the present only through heredity. The journey so carefully introduced in chs. 1–3 is now undertaken by the nation as a whole. It has a bearing on the present not through memory, but through national experience. The generations of Moab and Horeb are conflated, enabling the past to impact upon the present in a novel and vigorous way. In particular, as the people of God is seen as one across time and place, Horeb does not inform the present by the power of folklore, but through the corporate experience of the one people of God.

rehearsal of aspects of the tradition in chs. 1–3 is explicable, but that the list of events in 4.44-49 predated chs. 1–3, and was then expanded to form these chapters, is scarcely credible. Deut. 4.44-49 is a meaningful historical summary only in the light of the first three chapters of the book as we now have them.

Thus the revelation at Moab, the Mosaic preaching which ch. 4 introduces, is tied to that at Horeb by a formal legal designation and by the introduction of a concept of national solidarity which transcends the constraints of time and place.

Alongside the conflation of generations within the journey motif, there is a transition from a purely retrospective concern to one encompassing the future of Israel. The general principles set out in 4.25-31 are the natural development of the journey motif which is so prominent in chs. 1–3. The introduction of the distant future in the rhetorical scheme also anticipates much of the material to follow (see especially the blessings and curses, and chs. 29–30) and thus establishes ch. 4 as an overture to the rest of the book. The journey now extends through Egypt, Horeb, Moab, Canaan, 'Exile', and then back to the Land through repentance.

The theological use of the categories of time and place, introduced in chs. 1–3, is now developed. The role of Moab as the place of decision, the second Kadesh Barnea, is assumed throughout, but a further identification of Moab with Horeb, merely hinted at in chs. 1–3, is the focus of the chapter. The two events separated by forty years are collapsed into a single moment as Moses addresses the next generation as those who experienced the theophany firsthand. At every level Deuteronomy 4 is concerned with the response of Israel to Yahweh. There is significant contact with the rhetorical techniques and historical detail of chs. 1–3, although the subtle irony and careful construction of parallels has given way to a more direct approach. In addition, theological themes emerge which are expanded later in the book. When the theological coherence of the text is uncovered, it appears that this chapter can lay a substantial claim to being the hermeneutical key to Deuteronomic theology as displayed in the book as a whole.

### 3. *Time and Place in Chapters 5–11: The Journey of Israel in the Parenesis*

We have seen that the opening four chapters of Deuteronomy are concerned to demonstrate that the emergent nation of Israel has reached a crisis point in its short existence. At Moab God has presented them with the opportunity to reverse the disastrous repercussions of their refusal to enter Canaan from Kadesh Barnea. Chapter 4 suggests that this is to be realized by returning in some way to the formative moment of Israel as God's people—the revelation at Horeb. Chapters 5–11 include this foundational insight as a part of its parenetic armoury, to call Israel to a radical obedience with far-reaching consequences. In this section of the book the significance of today's decision at Moab expands to embrace a wealth of future possibilities.

### History of Interpretation

For the whole of this century the study of these chapters has been dominated by attempts to establish the literary and redaction history. The progress of the debate has been traced most comprehensively by Preuss.[71] It is neither desirable nor possible to examine the details of the individual attempts to account for these chapters of the book, varied and imaginative as they are, in any great detail. We can, however, point out the common problems and solutions which have lain at the centre of almost all recent work.

There is no consensus on the precise structure of the chapter, yet it is clear that ch. 5 stands apart in some way from what succeeds it. The first problem facing any examination of the text is providing an explanation for the inclusion of the Decalogue here, with the concomitant questions raised concerning its relationship to the Exodus version. Not surprisingly opinions are split regarding both the nature of the chapter itself and its incorporation into Deuteronomy. Further possible permutations are added by the various accounts of the relationship to Exodus 20. Even when dealing only with ch. 5, the complexities involved in a literary-critical study are obvious.

When coupled with the many variables in the interpretation of chs. 6–11, the number of possibilities arising in this type of study becomes vast. This is reflected in the number of careful and detailed literary theories which have been proposed in recent times. Lohfink's *Das Hauptgebot* was the first (and the most influential) of the latest studies. Many of its inadequacies have been pointed out, even by Lohfink himself, but it was an epoch-making work, whose combination of literary, redaction and form criticism laid the groundwork of much that followed. It is impossible to do justice to his careful argument in such a short space, but Lohfink's findings could be reduced in essence to the theory that early covenantal material was used by the Deuteronomist to expound the *Hauptgebot*, with editorial development over the years, resulting in the

---

71.   H.-D. Preuss, *Deuteronomium*, pp. 93-96. See also C. Brekelmans, 'Deut. 5', in *Das Deuteronomium* (ed. Lohfink), pp. 164-73.

careful balance of historical and parenetic sections we now find around this same central theme.While the findings of, for example, Seitz and Garcia Lopez differ, their methods remain essentially the same.[72]

It is strange that scholars who start from the same point, and use the same text and the same methodology, can obtain such wildly differing results. Such divergence arises through the inevitable subjective elements in literary analysis on both a macroscopic and microscopic scale—the variety of 'answers' obtained suggests that any literary study of these chapters must contain its fair share of educated guesses! On the grand scale most theories are based on a broad division of the text into two or more major layers. Lohfink, for example, begins by isolating the ancient covenantal material, by way of foundation for his detailed study, while Lopez first tries to separate the parenetic from the historical. The subjectivity in this large-scale process is scarcely diminished by the multitude of source- and redaction-critical questions to be answered for every pericope. Thus we have a new solution to correspond to each new study.

The concentration on source, redaction and literary–criticism in the study of Deuteronomy 5–11 has brought us to something of an impasse. It is not unfair to say also that the preoccupation with literary matters has resulted in the neglect of the *content* of these chapters. Theological comments are confined to concluding remarks, or brief asides.[73]

It is not the purpose of this essay to examine systematically the strengths and weaknesses of the host of studies of chs. 5–11. Instead I propose to study the rhetoric and theology of the text, particularly in view of the insights gleaned from the opening chapters. Such a study, I believe, is best suited to the articulation of the themes of time and place.

It would be an exaggeration to say that 'Time' and 'Place' are the controlling concepts at every point in the text. They do, however, provide a thread which runs throughout, and illuminate the central concerns

---

72. See *Das Hauptgebot*, pp. 289-91. He comments: 'Formulierung des Hauptgebots aus verschiedenen Zeiten und verschiedenen Traditionen bilden die Bauelemente des Textes. Doch auch als ganzer ist der Text in neuen Dimensionen dabei geblieben, das Hauptgebot im Menschen aufzurichten' (p. 285). F.G. Lopez, 'Analyse littéraire de Deut. 5–11', in *RB* 84 (1977), pp. 481-522 and 85 (1978), pp. 1-49; G. Seitz, *Redaktionsgeschichtliche Studien zum Deuteronomium* (BWANT, 93; Stuttgart: Kohlhammer, 1971).

73. E.g. Lopez's interesting assertion that 'le *Deutéronome primitif, l'alliance de l'Horeb*, et *l'alliance de Moab* font désormais partie du même ensemble littéraire' ('Analyse littéraire', p. 48) is carried no further.

of the parenesis of Deuteronomy 5–11, and its place in the book as a whole.

### Interpretation of Chapters 5–11

As we saw with ch. 4, there is a greater continuity between chs. 5–11 and the preceding material than is usually allowed. It is my proposal that this phase of the text should be read as an unbroken hortatory scheme, building on the theology of the opening four chapters.

Chapters 1–3 and 4 are, in many ways, distinct from the smooth rhetorical movement which can be seen in chs. 5–11. After the historical retrospect of the opening chapters, and the 'overture' of ch. 4, introducing far-reaching ideas which undergird every phase of the book, there seems to be a gradual change of genre.[74] We move into a sustained parenesis, encompassing many disparate elements, leading to the lawcode. However, this shift in genre is accompanied by a continuity of theme. We have already seen that ch. 4 extends the concept of the journey of Israel, applying it to the Israelites at Moab in terms of the Horeb theophany. Chapter 5 reiterates this, concentrating now on the parallel content of the revelation at Horeb and that at Moab. Chapters 6–11 pick up on this identification, while developing the distinctives of the parenesis, addressing the peculiar needs of the occupying 'force' in Canaan.

Our basic contention, then, is that the significance of time and place in this section of the book initially derives from ch. 4. The detailed rehearsal of the Decalogue in ch. 5 is carefully used to cement the link between the content of the Horeb revelation and the preaching of Moses at Moab, introduced in ch. 4. Chapter 6 sees another change in emphasis from retrospect to 'prospect' (cf. 4.25), as the focus shifts to the entry and occupation of the land. It is made clear that the response to the words of Moab will play a determinative role in the course of any attempted advance and establishment of a new national polity in the land. Chapters 7–11 move easily between the urgent requirements of Israel in the immediate future, often expressed in terms of the preoccupations of earlier chapters, and the long-term necessities of life in the land. The themes of time and place are consistently used in sharpening

---

74. In Deuteronomy it is often impossible to separate parenesis from history—as such it is not appropriate to detect well-defined boundaries between genres at every point in the book. Rather we have a flowing rhetorical unit, whose *emphasis* shifts in a way which is not easy to characterize by strict formal criteria.

the call to Israel to go forward as God's people. This thematic unity is one aspect of the unity in chs. 1–11 which is becoming increasingly apparent.

## Deuteronomy 5

Chapter 5 opens with five short verses of Moses' direct speech to all the people of Israel. Chapter 4 introduced the idea of the manner and content of the revelation at Horeb as determinative of the ongoing revelation at Moab, and concentrates on the implications of 'no image being seen'. Here it is the latter theme which takes precedence, with the emphasis shifting from the visible phenomena to the audible.

Initially the aim is to reiterate the identification made throughout ch. 4 (see e.g. 4.10) of the Horeb and Moab generations, and to sharpen the call to obey. Lohfink argues that this whole chapter is dominated by the formal characteristic which he designates 'Das paränetische Schema', which describes how the law must be fulfilled if blessing is to be enjoyed.[75] He is undoubtedly correct to highlight such a concern in this chapter. The weakness of his account lies in his failure to make clear that this message of obedient response in every situation is not restricted to formal characteristics, but is exhibited in every facet of the chapter, and belongs to the very heart of the Deuteronomic theology.

In 5.1 the link with ch. 4 becomes very obvious, as we encounter the 'laws and statutes' once more. It is important at this point to develop the earlier study of this phrase to encompass the whole of the parenesis, since it not only determines the nature of ch. 4, but reveals how the usage there shapes the Deuteronomic presentation of the Decalogue, the parenesis to follow, and the lawcode itself. In 5.1 the rehearsal of the Decalogue is prefaced by the now familiar החקים והמשפטים. The repetition of the phrase in 11.32 forms an inclusio around the parenesis introducing the lawcode proper. The relationship of 11.32 with what follows will be discussed in due course. It is evident that this use of החקים והמשפטים as *ein Struktursignal* has significance for how the material in chs. 5–11 is related to the lawcode proper.[76] It appears to suggest that

---

75. 'In der dt. Sprache ist das Schema so fest verankert, dass die Folge seiner Teile zu einem Denkablauf geworden ist, der auch in anderen Situationen, wenn es nicht formal um eine Ermahnung der Zuhörer zur Gesetzesbeobachtung geht, verwendet werden kann' (*Das Hauptgebot*, pp. 90; also 149, 151). Lohfink strongly defends the unity of the chapter.

76. Braulik, 'Die Ausdrücke', p. 62.

the 'law' of Deuteronomy encompasses the hortatory material as well as apodictic and casuistic law. This basic idea has already been suggested in the light of ch. 4. It also supports the theory that law in Deuteronomy is a developing concept, evolving in order to address new circumstances as they arise, in keeping with the ancient principles. In order to grasp the importance of the use of the phrase as an inclusio, however, we must appreciate the impact of each in context.

It is not hard to see that the primary reference of 5.1 is the Decalogue revealed to Moses by Yahweh on Horeb. Chapter 4 has introduced the Horeb theophany to the discussion as the ultimate source of authority for the 'laws and statutes'. Yet Deuteronomy 4 seems deliberately ambiguous concerning the exact content of these pronouncements. Sweeping statements about applicability for life in the land stand alongside appeals to the 'simple' Decalogue. Therefore the opening of ch. 5 comes as no surprise in one way—the laws and statutes are in fact equated with the Decalogue. Yet in the light of ch. 4 the laws and statutes simply cannot be restricted to a simple repetition of a previous revelation, no matter how seminal. There must be new legislation to come.

This ambivalence prepares the way for a further reference to החקים והמשפטים after the Decalogue in 5.31. The Decalogue is presented as the beginning of a process of declaration, not the end. Horeb is certainly the foundational moment for the constitution of Israel as the people of God—but if they are to continue to live as his people in their radically altered situation in Canaan, then this law must be built upon, as Yahweh continues to reveal his will at Moab. These chapters invest the ethics of Israel with a dynamic which is seldom appreciated.

The addition of the category 'all the command' in 5.31 is important. We have moved from a bipartite designation in 5.1 to a tripartite form in 5.31. There are two important implications of this. The first point to note is that the shift to the tripartite phrase supports the thesis that a development is in progress in the legislation of Israel. Initially the ten words are the 'laws and the statutes'. Now the 'laws and statutes' are joined by 'all the command'. This designates something additional and yet closely related to the Decalogue. It seems that החקים והמשפטים now encompasses the Decalogue, yet is not exhausted by a simple recitation. החקים והמשפטים is expanded to subsume the whole Deuteronomic parenesis, which stretches far beyond the end of ch. 5. The second vital feature is the introduction of a singular form alongside the more usual expression. This almost certainly emphasizes the coherence of the different aspects of the Deuteronomic proclamation. Brekelmans states,

> When the whole question of the relation between the Decalogue and the Deuteronomic law is eliminated, the meaning of the chapter and its place in Deuteronomy are anything but clear to me. Indeed the coherence of the whole chapter would be destroyed. [77]

The parenesis and the code to follow are of identical authority, and ultimately identical origin to the original חקים ומשפטים revealed at Horeb. The concept of law in Deuteronomy is thus much broader than the Decalogue, and it is this law which the rest of the book expounds. At 5.31, then, we are still waiting strictly for the *content* of the new revelation to begin. The preamble of chs. 4–5 has been concerned with demonstrating the continuity of the new with the old. The phrase the 'laws and statutes' has been used with an air of vagueness, to facilitate the new dynamism in the Deuteronomic view of law, and to create an air of tense expectation as the book unfolds.

The reference to החקים והמשפטים in 5.31 is closely linked to that in 6.1.[78] This underlines that the Decalogue in ch. 5 is not the final word on the law in the eyes of the Deuteronomist. The possibility of extension of the laws for life in the land introduced in 5.31 becomes a reality in ch. 6. Once again the tripartite expression is used to emphasize the continuity and development of this legislative programme. Deut. 6.1 and 5.31 belong together. The repetition of the phrase in 6.1 increases the momentum of the 'snowball' considerably. Now there can be no doubt that the law in Deuteronomy is widening its scope to include elements not normally classified as such. The significance and positioning of 6.4 now become more comprehensible in the context of the whole book. At

---

77. 'Deuteronomy 5', p. 167.

78. See Lohfink, *Das Hauptgebot*, p. 151, for the chiastic structure bridging the transition between chs. 5 and 6, and for a discussion of the overall unity of the chapters. Also: 'Das in 6.2a durch die palindromische Bewegung anklingende Dekalogthema wird mit dem Gesetzthema verbunden: der Dekalogterminus aus 5.29 bildet eine Reihe mit *hahuqqot*, sonst einem Gesetzesterminus, so dass *miswotayw* hier zwar alle Gesetze, nicht nur den Dekalog meint, auf diesen aber dennoch mitanspielt. Der Bezug zwischen den *huqqim umispatim* und dem Dekalog wird auf diese Weise noch einmal herausgestellt. Dieser Ausdruck determiniert die *miswa* im Sinne einer authorativen Gesetzsammlung von Rechtsbestimmungen (*huqqim*) die das vom Dekalog her offen Bleibende klärt (*mispatim*)' ('Die *huqqim umispatim*', p. 9).

the heart of the Deuteronomic development is the emphatic insistence
that keeping the law is not merely a matter of external obedience, but
attitude. The ringing tones of the Shema can then logically take their
place at the beginning of the 'new' material to go under the rubric of
החקים והמשפטים. The decision to love Yahweh without constraint is then
the dominant theme of the following chapters.

The other occurrences of החקים והמשפטים in the body of the
*Hauptgebotsparänese* come in 6.20 and 7.11. In context both
re-emphasize the intricate link between the events of the Exodus, and
preeminently the events at Horeb, with the exposition on the plains of
Moab. The tripartite expression in 6.20 is identical to that in 4.45.
Lohfink maintains that in both places only העדת is original, but this is
extremely speculative. Deut. 7.11 echoes the form of 5.31 and 6.1. Both
these verses underline the basic message that the Deuteronomic
'preached law' is expanding on and in continuity with the Horeb tradition. The reaffirmations occur here in a didactic context, rather than as
markers of structure and thus theme.

I have already mentioned 11.32 as forming an *inclusio* with 5.1 for
the parenesis preceding the lawcode. It cannot be separated either from
the following verse, which acts as the heading for the code, as the
briefest glance will reveal. Seitz has pointed out the chiastic arrangement
running through 11.31–12.1.[79] Even so, 11.26-32 is delineated as a unit
in itself by the repetition of 'I am giving you/ am about to give you this
day'. There is a very definite new beginning, and yet this new phase of
החקים והמשפטים cannot be separated from what has gone before. This
device forges a link between the lawcode and the parenesis of chs. 6–11.
But it does more than that—it ties the legal stipulations of chs. 12–26
inextricably to the long meditation on the need for obedience to be
rooted in love, and beyond that to the Decalogue itself. The lawcode is
to be understood as 'the laws and statutes' in the same way as both the
Decalogue and the preaching of chs. 6–11. To get to the root of this
relationship is to understand the heart of Deuteronomic theology. Here
the ethical agenda of the Deuteronomist is clearly exposed.

It seems that there is an unbroken theme running through the book
from ch. 4 to the Decalogue in ch. 5 and the parenesis of chs. 6–11, to
the lawcode of 12–26.[80] The concluding passage of the Lawcode

---

79. Seitz, *Studien*, p. 39. See also McConville, *Law and Theology in
Deuteronomy* (JSOTSup, 33; Sheffield: JSOT Press, 1984), ch 2.
80. See S.A. Kaufmann, 'The Structure of the Deuteronomic Law', *Maarav* 1/2

supplies further evidence for such an understanding of the laws (26.16–17). The Code is concluded with both a reminder of the link with the Decalogue, which is particularly evident in the well-worn designation, and by the appended motivation appealing directly to the opening passage of the parenesis of ch. 6. Verse 17 sets all of this in the context of decision, the category above all others which seems to characterize the motivation for the Deuteronomist's choice of material, style and presentation. It is interesting that here alone המצוה is inserted in the middle of החקים והמשפטים. No ready explanation for this is available, other than as a device to illustrate the inseparability of the categories.[81]

On the understanding set out in detail above, the Deuteronomic law cannot be separated from the Deuteronomic ethos—the phrase החקים והמשפטים encompasses the theological affirmations required, the attitudes fostered, the emotions stirred and the response set out in the legislation. The three main phases of the book are carefully and intricately linked with one another. The parenesis is presented as the inevitable product of the revelation at Horeb. The Lawcode is the result of a reapplication of the model of life given at Horeb for the new circumstances in the life of the nation becoming visible on the threshold of the land. It appears that this examination of the phrase החקים והמשפטים has strengthened the case for regarding ch. 4 as intrinsically linked to the hortatory and legal material which follows in chs. 5–26. Chapter 4 is crucial to the development of the theological perspectives of the rest of the book, and seems to be the point from which the Deuteronomic distinctives emanate. Only when the deliberate fusion of ideas exhibited by the use of this crucial phrase in chs. 5–11 is understood, can the real force of the parenesis be grasped.

Returning to the discussion of ch. 5, I must begin by commenting on 5.2-3. The significance of these verses is often passed over, but within the Deuteronomic scheme it is crucial—the ethical impact of the Mosaic preaching to follow seems to be contingent upon the twin events of Horeb and Moab involving the same people, the same God and

(1978/79), pp. 105-58; Braulik, 'Die Abfolge der Gesetze in Deuteronomium 12-26 und der Dekalog', in *Das Deuteronomium* (ed. Lohfink), pp. 252-72, and *Die deuteronomischen Gesetze und der Dekalog* (SBS, 145; Stuttgart: Katholisches Bibelwerk, 1991). This question is also considered in some detail in Millar, *Ethics*.

81. It should be noted at this point that as the book progresses it is in fact המצוה which becomes the dominant term for covering the whole of the Deuteronomic preaching—see 6.25; 8.1; 11.8, 22; 15.5; 17.20; 19.9; 27.1; 30.11; 31.5.

essentially the same revelation. The Moab generation are assumed to have experienced the Horeb theophany. Once more this is not merely an anachronism, but part of a carefully conceived theological scheme. In v. 3 the correspondence between Horeb and Moab is made totally explicit—the current generation is not to think of the covenant at Horeb as a mere memory, but as *a memory which is actualized in the present at Moab*.[82] Miller helpfully points out the 'insistence on the contemporaneity of the covenant' and comments,

> This verse expresses a kind of hermeneutical formula for the book. The time gap and the generation gap are dissolved in the claim that the covenant at Sinai, the primal revelation that created the enduring relationship between the people and the Lord was really made with the *present* generation. The covenant is not an event, a claim, a relationship of the past; it is of the present. The time between the primal moment and the present moment is telescoped, and the two are equated.[83]

Moses claims that the central element of the national experience at Horeb was Yahweh addressing the nation 'face to face'. Some have perceived a difficulty here. There is no explicit mention of a direct revelation of the Ten Commandments to the whole people 'face to face' in Exodus 20, which is more in keeping with the affirmation of Mosaic mediation in v. 5.[84] This tension has led many to assign v. 4 to a later hand. No such measure is necessary. Deuteronomy 5 is not concerned to paint a detailed picture of the theophany at Sinai. The 'mechanics' of the encounter are irrelevant at this point. The crucial element is that Yahweh spoke to the people in a way which no-one could miss.

---

82.  Also von Rad: 'In view of Deut. 2.14ff. we are surprised by the remark that this covenant was made not with an earlier generation but with those who are now alive. Even though the death of the Sinai generation had occurred meanwhile and lay outside the speaker's view, his intention is clear enough. He wants to bring the event of the covenant-making which already belongs to the past vividly before the eyes of his contemporaries (cf. a similar procedure in 29.13-14). These are the words of a generation which must begin by providing itself with an explanation of its relation to the 'saving event' (Heilsereignis)', *Deuteronomy*, p. 55.

83.  P.D. Miller, *Deuteronomy*, p. 67.

84.  I.e. whether the divine voice was instantly understandable, or required 'translation'. At this point the Deuteronomist has no interest in giving a blow by blow account of events—contrast Exod. 20 (the temporal reference of Exod. 20.18-22 is a little uncertain, and does not in fact necessarily contradict anything described in Deuteronomy). See E.W. Nicholson, 'The Decalogue as the Direct Address of God', *VT* 27 (1977), pp. 422-33.

Alongside this he affirms his own role in mediating the content of the revelation to the Israelites. Both of these are essential to the thought of the chapter; Yahweh communicated in an unmistakable way and Moses conveyed the details to the people.

The narrative is ordered in this way for a precise theological purpose: to claim that the words of Moses carry exactly the same authority today at Moab as they did immediately after the theophany at Horeb. Forty years (and an entire generation) may have passed, but in the divine economy *all* Israel has experienced theophany, hearing the voice of God firsthand, and now must continue to respond to the words of Moses, his spokesman.

Just such an understanding is evident in vv. 22-27. Yahweh spoke to *all* Israel decisively from the fire and cloud declaring the commandments to them, and 'then said no more'. This distinct revelation was then succeeded by communication via a mediator. This communal experience constitutive of the nation was augmented by the intimate revelations of Yahweh to Moses on behalf of the nation. The most notable feature of these verses is the preponderance of references to the 'voice of Yahweh'. I would suggest that the concentration on this aspect of the theophany at this point is a deliberate device to strengthen the identification of Moab and Horeb. At both places Israel hears the voice of God. At Horeb Israel encountered Yahweh in an intimate and overwhelming way. In both the Exodus and Deuteronomic traditions this direct experience of God is halted at the request of the people, and replaced by a mediated revelation (cf. Exod. 20.19). Moab now represents the continuation of this mediated revelation.

Deuteronomy 5 suggests that the experience of the Israelites at Moab subsumes and augments that at Horeb. Not only were this generation 'at Horeb', but they have seen so much more of Yahweh in action since. In response to this, they must obey the divine word, as transmitted by Moses. Verse 31 ascribes the same divine origin to the Mosaic preaching at Moab as that at Horeb; vv. 32-33 make clear that the same obedience is required of Israel.

Thus the significance of the Decalogue in Deuteronomy is not merely a historical one. Israel is not simply called to remember the content of the revelation at Horeb and adhere to it. Something much more profound is happening. Israel is assumed to have experienced the self-disclosure of Yahweh at Horeb, and is expected to respond to *this* revelation by obeying the specific terms of the continuing Mosaic commands, the new revelation at Moab. The preaching of Moses redefines the demands of 'Horeb-moment' in terms of the 'Moab-moment' in Israel's present experience.

Horeb takes its place alongside Kadesh Barnea as one of the arche-typal points of decision faced by Israel in the past—the very mention of Horeb summed up both the gracious acts of Yahweh in leading the nation out of Israel, and the response he desired and facilitated by revealing his will to Moses at this place of command. Thus taking the nation back to meditate on the Horeb tradition has the effect of presenting them with a further choice—not only do they have to decide whether or not to enter the land (as at Kadesh Barnea), but they must choose the foundations upon which they build their new life in the land, in the light of their encounter with Yahweh himself.

### Deuteronomy 6

Chapter 6 marks a distinct shift in the rhetorical focus of Deuteronomy. In the first five chapters, while references to the future of Israel are not excluded, there is a distinct emphasis on informing present decisions from past experience. After the detailed examination of the lessons of Horeb for the nation waiting at Moab, preparing them for the new reve-lation of the divine word, the possibilities and problems of the future begin to dominate the discussion.

Moab is the fulcrum of the history of Israel in the view of Deuteronomy. The past, present and future of the nation are intimately tied to Moab, the place of decision. We have already seen that Moab is the *place of recapitulation*—now it becomes also the *place of anticipation*.[85]

Both of these designations warrant further comment. In chs. 1–5 Moab is carefully presented as the culmination of Israelite history, as missed opportunities are reversed, and Yahweh speaks again. As the place of recapitulation Moab could be described as both the place of revelation (the new Horeb) and the place of action (the new Kadesh Barnea). In ch. 6 further dimensions to the decisions facing Israel at Moab are spelled out. 'Today' the chance is given not merely to undo the mistakes of the past, but to realize the potential of an exciting future. As the place of anticipation Moab is the place of entry to the land, the place at which Israel must stay 'spiritually' to occupy the land, and the

85. In Brueggemann's terminology ('Imagination as a mode of fidelity') these could be considered as the places of memory and imagination respectively.

place to which it must return in her spiritual journey if she is to return to the land after apostasy (see especially chs. 4 and 30).

There is a strong element of continuity between chs. 4, 5 and 6 at a formal, rhetorical and theological level, which has important implications for the interpretation of the text. The different aspects of the role of Moab can be represented diagrammatically as follows:

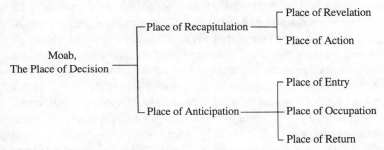

Chapter 6 ties together Moab as holding the key to entering the land, and to a successful occupation of it.

The role of Moab in the entry into the land is closely linked to the idea of Moab as a second Kadesh Barnea, but now it is the impending possibilities which fill the frame rather than past failures. It is shown most clearly in the injunctions to 'obey these statutes...*so that you may go into the land to inherit it*'. This idea has already occurred in 4.1 and 5.30, but it is only in ch. 6 that it becomes prominent (see 6.1, 18, 24).[86]

We must be careful, however, not to reduce the Deuteronomic perception of Moab to merely that of a door to the land, for the significance of Moab as a place stretches on into Israel's future. This is made clear in 6.1-3 (cf. 11.8-9), where the writer moves naturally from Moab as holding the key to entry to its significance for continued occupation.

The motif of long life inevitably extends the decision from the present moment to a perpetual lifestyle in the future. Life for Israel is to be life at Moab, even when firmly rooted in Canaan.[87]

86. See also 8.1, 7-8; 9.4-6; 10.11; 11.8-9, 22, 23; 16.20, and variations on this theme. This idea is not unique to Deuteronomy—see Pss. 37.11, 22, 29, 34; Prov. 2.21-2; 10.30.

87. This is consistent with the concern that Israel should never forget what Yahweh has done—see e.g. 4.25, 8.10-20. On this view, forgetting Yahweh is tantamount to forgetting the decisions faced and made at Moab, and turning from the life of decision (which by definition must be a life of uncertainty and dependence) to a life of complacency, betraying an underlying pride of achievement. It has been pointed

Alternatively this could be expressed in terms of life on the move. Israel's journey does not stop on settling in the land—they are always on the verge of new possibilities, whose realization depends on learning from past experience. The dynamic of life at this point of decision at Moab is clearly visible too in 6.1-3, 24-25. Examples of this understanding proliferate in the extended sermonic section leading to the lawcode, e.g. 7.12-14, 8.10-20, 11.13-21, as we shall see. (The lawcode itself provides an even stronger basis for understanding the ongoing life of Israel as life at 'Moab' the place of occupation. The lawcode obviously presupposes the occupation of Canaan, and legislates for the life of a settled, expanding community).

At times then, it seems that obedience at Moab is the condition for entry to Canaan, whereas elsewhere this is taken for granted and obedience is necessary only for enjoyment of blessing in the land. This takes us into a broader area than the significance of Moab—that of the land itself. I discuss the significance of the land in Deuteronomic theology in detail in my thesis, and McConville deals with land terminology in relation to the 'place-formula' elsewhere in this volume. While in one sense the land is the place *par excellence* in the book, and of crucial importance, a general treatment of the theme would take us far beyond the remit of this study. I will confine myself to exegetical comment.

In ch. 6 itself, it is clear that the preaching of Moses exploits the tension between the land as gift and the accompanying responsibility to obey to the full—building his imperatives into his exposition of the indicatives. Moab takes it place in this scheme as the place of decision which will determine both successful conquest and survival in the land of promise. Thus recognizing this fundamental duality in the significance of Moab is not a piece of theological chicanery. On the contrary it is a result of the subtle interaction of grace and law, the indicatives and the imperatives in the message of the book, which is always concerned to urge Israel on to obedience and blessing.

Thus Moab stands at the theological intersection of both the Deuteronomic doctrines of promise and obedience, as well as at the temporal intersection of past and future. It is then in the context of Moab, as the place of recapitulation and anticipation, the place of promise and obedience, that the Shema should surely be understood.

out that this assertion is very difficult to disprove exegetically. This stems from the cumulative nature of the argument, rather than any inherent weakness in the case which has been presented.

The call to Israel to 'hear' is usually designated as an appeal to wisdom language, and is passed over without further comment. Several features of the text suggest that this is not satisfactory.

First, there is the repeated occurrence of שמע as a *Leitwort* throughout chs. 4 and 5, in the extended treatment of Israel 'hearing' Yahweh's voice in the Horeb theophany, and its identification with the Mosaic preaching to follow. In addition Lohfink has shown in some detail the linguistic connections between the conclusion of ch. 5 and the beginning of ch. 6. Even in 6.3 the call to 'hear' is explicit. The import of the Shema in 6.4 then *cannot* be understood if it is stripped from its immediate context in 6.1-4, and its general context stretching back to 4.1.

Deut. 6.1-4 binds the entry to the land and the enjoyment of the land to an appropriate, obedient response to the word of Yahweh, heard by Israel at Horeb and now declared by Moses at Moab. The call to 'hear' then takes Israel simultaneously back to Horeb and forward into Canaan. In many ways it could be described as the turning-point of the parenesis. Repeatedly the fact that Israel 'heard' Yahweh speak at Horeb has been underlined, and it is implicit that Israel must go on 'hearing' these words—now in exactly the same way Israel is urged to 'hear' the voice at Moab.[88] The only difference is that the words of Yahweh are now identified as the preaching of Moses. The call to 'hear' is a command to meet with God and to credit Moses' new words with the same divine origin as the Decalogue itself. Past and future coalesce in this moment of absolute significance at Moab. The Shema affirms the Decalogue, and then points to an exposition and reapplication of these 'Words' for the new conditions of conquest and occupation of Canaan.

Without chs. 4 and 5, then, the Shema is cut loose from its moorings and its basic meaning. Or looking at it from another perspective, the Shema affirms the theological coherence of chs. 4–6.

Deut. 6.10-11 goes on to describe the fulfilment of the promise of Abraham in terms of an 'urban Eden': v. 11 recalls the Exodus, v. 16 the rebellion at Massah—all so that Israel 'may enter and occupy the land' (v. 18). The past and the future are inextricably linked. So are the promise and obedience. The entry and the occupation may be spoken of separately, but ultimately the key to both is 'hearing the voice of Yahweh' at Horeb, Moab and on into the land.

---

88. The Shema makes this clear by summarizing the Decalogue as it points forward to the Moasaic preaching.

In all this the significance of Moab itself is a little puzzling. There is little evidence of any interest in discovering the precise setting of the Mosaic discourse either inside or outside the Canon. Moab itself gets a reasonable degree of attention in the Old Testament, but almost all of this is condemnatory. So why the concentration on Moab in the preaching of Moses?

The answer is probably very simple. George Adam Smith pointed out the geographical suitability for Moab as a place from which to survey the land.[89] The point is not that the place at which Israel is to live is *Moab per se*, but rather that Israel is to live at this moment in their national experience, looking back to the past and on to the possibilities of their relationship with Yahweh in the land. Neither Horeb nor Moab was destined to become a place of pilgrimage. Both, however, were places of huge spiritual importance in the journey of Israel. In each case the significance derived solely from the revelation received. It was imperative that Israel 'stayed' at Horeb, in the sense of appropriating its lessons into the national consciousness, while moving on towards the land (1.6). In the same way Israel had to 'stay' at Moab as the nation took possession of Canaan.

It may be accidental, but it is striking that this idea of successive places where Israel knew Yahweh's intimate, revealing presence seems in direct contrast to the usual understanding of the altar-law in ch. 12. Rather than any concern to localize worship at a sanctuary, the parenesis focuses on Yahweh's presence with Israel at various crucial stages on its journey. Yahweh is free to move on, and Israel must move with him. It is hard to avoid making a connection with the Deuteronomic desire to point Israel away from the Canaanite practice of 'tying' deities to a single location to a vision of a transcendent God who remains immanent where his people are.[90]

The significance of both Horeb and Moab in Deuteronomy lies not in the places themselves, not even as places of revelation or theophany to be marked, but as reminders that, in contrast to the gods of the

---

89.    G.A. Smith, *The Historical Geography of the Holy Land* (London: Hodder & Stoughton, 25th edn, 1931), ch. XXVII, see esp. pp. 592-93. From the plateau of Moab 'The whole of the Jordan valley is now open from Engedi, beyond which the mists become impenetrable, to where, on the north, the hills of Gilead seem to meet those of Ephraim. The Jordan flows below: Jericho is visible beyond. Over Gilead Hermon can be seen in clear weather...'

90.    Once again see McConville on this concept.

Canaanites, God is transcendent, and must be heard in every place and in every situation.

Chapter 6 makes the transition from the identification of Moab with Horeb to the crucial importance of Moab for the future of Israel in Canaan. The implications of the decisions faced at Moab for entering and occupying the land are then addressed at some length in the remainder of the parenetic section. Now that the significance of 'today at Moab' has been established, there is clearly less need to make explicit reference to times and places in chs. 7–11. However not only does such thinking undergird the progress of the exhortations, but it emerges into full view at several key points.

## Deuteronomy 7–11

Chapter 7 consists of a thorough treatment of the problem of the current occupants of the land. There have been numerous attempts to establish the links between Exodus 23, 34, Joshua 2 and this chapter. These will not be discussed here.[91] The problem, however, constituted the first concrete decision which Israel was to face on 'entering and occupying' Canaan (see 7.1, 8.1, 9.1 etc.). As such it falls easily into the logical progression of the rhetoric of these chapters. Verses 1-5 provide a clear statement of the action which must be taken (cf. chs. 12 and 13, and Exod. 34.13-17) and v. 6 the rationale. Verses 11-16 emphasize that this is to be understood in the context of obedience at Moab—the place which enables successful occupation as set out in ch. 6. The 'Holy War' cannot be undertaken without reference to the commands of Yahweh given at Horeb and now 'updated' at Moab.

The stereotyped opening of ch. 8 underlines the continuity of theme in this section of the book. The exposition of the heart of the parenesis, the decision at Moab, continues. Once more past experience and future possibility converge at Moab. Verses 1-5 remind Israel of the educative events of the wilderness,[92] and vv. 7-10 point to the potential of the future. It is in view of both of these that the powerful plea to remember Yahweh at all times is introduced in vv. 11-18. This material has much in common with 6.10-19. The stern warning of the consequences of failing to heed the injunctions at Moab brings the chapter to a close.

The repetition of the command to 'hear' in 9.1 may be intended to

91. But see Preuss's summary: *Deuteronomium*, pp. 101-103.

92. Which Lohfink neatly describes as a kind of experiment which revealed the love of God (*Das Hauptgebot*, p. 191).

reinforce the connection between Moab and Horeb. Since there is no explicit evidence of this in the text, we cannot be totally sure. In 9.2-3 the call to hear and advance is backed up by an assertion that Anakites pose no problem to Yahweh—in other words the people of Israel have every reason to trust Yahweh's command to go forward, in stark (and obvious) contrast to the costly failure to do just that at Kadesh Barnea. The identification of Moab as the place of action and revelation detected in chs. 1–5 is also clear here. It is developed at some length from 9.1–10.11. Braulik, Mayes and Lohfink all regard this passage as post-exilic, linking it to the perspective of chs. 1–3. If it is accepted, as I have argued, that chs. 1–3 are an intrinsic part of the Deuteronomic parenesis, then it becomes particularly difficult to sustain this on the basis of the text alone.

In v. 7 the wilderness is presented as a vivid example of Yahweh's care of Israel (cf. 8.2-4), and Horeb as the ultimate proof of Israel's stubborn rejection of Yahweh. Even here, at the place of revelation *par excellence*, the people of Israel did not respond to Yahweh as they ought. Five times in this long section Moses refers to 'forty days and forty nights' on Horeb (9.9, 11, 18, 25; 10.10). Weinfeld argues that this formula is of liturgical significance, marking the division of the section into smaller units.[93] The occurrences may have a structural function, but would seem to have an even more important rhetorical role. In the context of the stubbornness and apostasy of Israel it may well be that such frequent reminders of 'forty days and forty nights' of intimate fellowship with God would stand in sharp contrast to the forty years of discipline experienced by the nation in the wilderness.

In the middle of this long rehearsal of the Golden Calf incident, which serves as a stern warning to Israel of the potential of a place of revelation to become a place of apostasy, there comes a parenthesis in 9.22-24. If the evidence of the rebellion of Horeb was not sufficient to convince Israel of her tendency to rebel, then the events of Taberah, Massah, Kibroth-hattaavah and ultimately Kadesh Barnea itself must surely force the nation to face up to its delinquency. In the short distance (1.2) between Horeb and Kadesh the Israelites had managed to compound the apostasy at Horeb with a repeated refusal to trust Yahweh's provision, whether of comfort (Taberah), water (Massah), manna (Kibroth-hattaavah), or even of the land of Canaan itself. Moab was potentially a place of great evil, as well as great blessing.

93. *Deuteronomy 1–11*, p. 427.

In 10.1-11 the second chance given to Israel at Sinai is narrated. Despite the most serious rejection of Yahweh, he revealed his word to them once again and provided not only a new set of tablets, but set apart a tribe to handle the ark (v. 8). This feature of the tradition is not introduced by accident. Rather as the parenesis reaches its climax it gives another example of the grace of Yahweh in giving Israel another chance. Moab was to be understood as a second Kadesh—another chance to occupy the land. But Israel should not be surprised at this— even at Horeb Israel received exactly such an opportunity. Moab shares not only *revelation* with Horeb, but also the demonstration of Yahweh's grace and forgiveness in providing his people with another chance to hear his word and experience the fulfilment of his promise.

One further comment should be made on the heavily marked command in Deut. 10.11. We have reached in many ways the end of the novel parenetic material. 10.12-22 acts as a short summary for chs. 9 and 10, and ch. 11 as a more developed conclusion to at least 5–10, and probably to 1–10 as a whole. It is interesting that the climax to the reversal of the complex of events at Horeb is the resumption of the journey of Israel (cf. 1.6-7). This journey is depicted as a response to the grace of Yahweh, and as it stands implies that there is a close link between the journey and the lawcode to which these chapters serve as an introduction. This short statement moves Israel back to Moab from the narrative setting at Horeb, while reminding them of the imminent departure which Yahweh has commanded them to make.

Chapter 11 serves as a summary and climax of all the material in the preceding ten chapters.[94] 'Today' at Moab is presented as the culmination of the events in Egypt and the wilderness (vv. 2-6). The novel element of the deaths of Dathan and Abiram is introduced for a very definite purpose. The account of the story in Num. 16.12-14 makes the sin committed quite explicit—they rejected Canaan in favour of Egypt:

> The narrative of the exodus and its aftermath recalled in 11.3-7 deliber-
> ately contrasts what God did for his people and what they did to him in
> return. He delivered them but they rebelled against him. In that story,

---

94. Lohfink, in *Das Haupotgebot*, pp. 102-103, tries to argue that 'Decalogue language' is missing from 10.12–11.32, and thus to drive a wedge between this section of the text and what has gone before. It is hard to see the force of this. If, on the other hand, 10.12–11.32 is seen as a double summary of the preceding material, one would expect some slight difference in the vocabulary and expression while observing a definite continuity of theme. This is what we observe.

Dathan and Abiram described Egypt, not Canaan as 'a land flowing with milk and honey'.[95]

Once again the generation at Moab is spoken of as having experienced the whole gamut of Israelite history, and thus have every reason to respond in the way prescribed. In vv. 8-17 the familiar theme of obedience at Moab holding the key to successful entry to and occupation of the land reappears, coupled with descriptions of Canaan in paradisal terms and severe warnings to deal radically with the Canaanites. Verses 18-25 return to the language of ch. 6 to underline the importance of absorbing the Mosaic preaching and acting upon it for the entire course of the nation's future.

As is typical in Deuteronomy, the section concludes with a new element—this time a graphic illustration of what it means to live at the point of decision both inside and outside the land. First in vv. 26-28 the choice before the people at Moab is characterized as one between blessing and curse. This is then translated physically to a new situation within the land itself at Shechem (v. 29). Here in the heart of the land, Israel is to re-enact the decision of Moab. These twin peaks would forever stand before Israel as a reminder of their dilemma on the verge of the land, and the continual obligation to decide for Yahweh, to choose blessing if they are to enjoy life with their God in it.

*Conclusion*

The insight of Deuteronomy 4 that the content of the revelation at Horeb is linked to the Mosaic preaching at Moab is developed at some length in ch. 5. Moab is the place where God can be heard to speak again as he spoke at Horeb. Chapter 5 is in turn linked inextricably to ch. 6, and in particular the Shema, as the focus shifts from the past to the future. The repetition of the phrase החקים והמשפטים reflects this theological connection at a formal level.

The reaction of the Israelites at this new place of revelation has even more significance than that at the mountain of God. Now the conquest and settlement of Canaan is at stake, as well as the development of the relationship with Yahweh. Moab is the place of recapitulation, bringing together the earlier opportunities and mistakes of Israel, but it is also the place of anticipation which holds the key to the national future. Moab becomes the locus for the expression of obedience of Israel, the nation

---

95.  R. Brown, *The Message of Deuteronomy* (Leicester: IVP, 1993), p. 138.

chosen by God to be holy. Dispossession of the Canaanite nations, cultivation of the land and future residence in Canaan all hinge on the obedience defined at Moab. As the parenesis moves to its climax it becomes increasingly apparent that Moab is the place which subsumes all previous places in Israel's past, and controls every dimension of Israel's future.

Moab thus takes its place in the scheme of the journey of Israel, opening the way for a life of blessing in the land—a life of remembering the acts of Yahweh and responding to them, a life of perpetually choosing the way of obedience—a 'settled-nomadism' which guarantees unbroken experience of the fulfilment of the promises of God, from Horeb to the land. Nowhere is this shown so clearly as in Deut. 10.11. At the conclusion of the parenesis the command to move on into the land is reiterated in identical terms to 1.6-7. Israel is a nation on the move with Yahweh—but only through obedience can any momentum be achieved and sustained.

### 4. *Time and Place in Chapters 27–34: The End of Many Journeys*

The aim of the concluding part of this essay is to show that the final phase of Deuteronomy in fact demonstrates the same concerns as the rest of the framework, *viz* the use of geographical and temporal ideas to urge Israel to make a faithful response to the covenant instituted by Yahweh. Studies of this part of the book are rather more sparse than in other areas, and few have attempted to investigate its theological relationship to all that precedes. As a result there is little need to provide any orientation to the present state of study, merely to interact with particular proposals in a rather *ad hoc* fashion.

#### The Literary Structure of Chapters 27–34

One of the major problems has been determining the relationship of the various pericopes to one another—for example, the blessings and curses of ch. 27 and the extended list of curses in ch. 28, the reference of 28.69 (29.1), and the role and nature of chs. 32 and 33. The concept of the journey of Israel in covenant faithfulness through Time and Place provides a new way of understanding connections and purpose in the conclusion to the book.

My own division of the text is as follows:

| I | 27.1-10 | The Stones and Altar on Mt Ebal |
| II | 27.11-26 | The Levitical Curses |
| III | 28.1-68 | Blessings and Curses on Gerizim/Ebal |
| IV | 28.69–29.29 | The Covenant at Moab |
| V | 30.1-10 | After the Curse—Return from 'Exile' |
| VI | 30.11-20 | Parenetic Climax |

Postscript

| VII | 31.1-8 | Succession of Joshua |
| VIII | 31.9-13 | Writing and Reading the Law |
| IX | 31.14–32.44 | Moses' Swan Song |
| X | 32.44–34.12 | The Death of Moses |

The most satisfactory way to treat these chapters is in individual units, examining how, if at all, the ideas of time and place exhibited in earlier parts of the book influence the presentation of its conclusion.

### I. *The Stones and Altar on Mount Ebal (27.1-10)*

After the conclusion of the lawcode, the text reverts to a third person prescription of actions to be carried out on entering the land. This has been interpreted by many as a literary discontinuity, and is used to argue that ch. 27 is unconnected to both chs. 26 and 28. It is often suggested that simply omitting this chapter produces a smooth narrative transition. This view has remained the consensus for most of this century. Such attempts to assign it to a late (and peripheral) layer of the book have been bolstered by the fact that the text as it stands is a massive problem for the theory that Deuteronomy is the ideological pillar supporting the Josianic demand for centralization of the sanctuary at Jerusalem. The literary-critical solutions to the roughness of this chapter are beyond the scope of our discussion.[96]

Anbar, however, does make one very interesting suggestion. He tries to show that the construction of the altar has been interpolated here to underline the parallels between the covenant at Shechem in Joshua 24 and that at Horeb. His basic insight is valid—that there is a connection between the two covenants. Shechem and Horeb are both places of covenant-making, and of ethical demands made on Israel. We have seen already, however, that reaching such a conclusion does not require a complicated comparison of pericopes in Joshua and Deuteronomy, but is in fact demanded by the logic of the book of Deuteronomy itself.

96. See M. Anbar, 'The Story of the Building of an Altar on Mount Ebal', in *Das Deuteronomium* (ed. Lohfink), pp. 304-10, for a summary.

Shechem is simply presented as the next place on the itinerary of the journey of Israel. Shechem is the inevitable successor to Moab, which in turn stood in continuity with Horeb. This simple explanation is more than adequate to account for the text.

Deuteronomy 27 begins with both a familiar element and a completely new one. The phrase 'all the commandment' is one of the hallmarks of the book, and implies a large degree of continuity with the concerns of both 1–11 and the lawcode to present Deuteronomy as a unified whole.[97] This similarity is reflected in a comparison of the verses which open ch. 27 and those which close ch. 11. It was argued that the extrapolation of the principle of decision in the life of Israel to the land was the logical climax of the exhortation of the first eleven chapters. It is also the only fitting response to the Code which has just been adumbrated.

The addition of the 'elders of Israel' to the ascription heading this section is unique (yet it finds a parallel in v. 11 with Moses and the 'levitical priests').[98] Irrespective of the origins of such a heading, it serves the rhetorical purpose of emphasizing the responsibility of the whole community to answer Yahweh's command in a decisive way. This is in keeping with the unparalleled cultic and covenantal demands made in the remainder of the chapter.

Much of the confusion surrounding this passage arises from the odd placement of v. 8. It seems that the initial command to set up the stones is completed in the repetitive vv. 2-4.[99] Yet we return to this theme in v. 8. One other problem with the text as it stands is the reference to 'the day when you cross into the land' in v. 2. It has been argued that Ebal is more than a day's journey from the crossing-point into the land, and that ביום cannot be restricted to a general sense.[100] In view of the use of temporal language in Deuteronomy as a whole, this objection is not

---

97. See 5.31; 6.25; 8.1; 11.8, 22; 15.5; 19.9; also 6.1; 7.11; 11.28.

98. It also mirrors the devolution of judicial power in ch. 1. There, however, the concern was to establish the culpability of the nation as a whole—here it is to underline the future responsibility of both elders and people in the land.

99. One small problem is the reference of the phrase 'all the words of this law' in v. 3. We have already seen the fluidity of the Deuteronomic concept of law (see the discussion on ch. 4 above), and it is difficult to determine if it refers to chs. 1–26, 12–26, or even to ch. 27. This is a perplexing puzzle, but one which does not impinge directly on our findings; the crucial point is that some of the Moab revelation is to be written down on stone just as at Horeb.

100. Mayes, *Deuteronomy*, pp. 340-41.

compelling. The concern of Moses is not with the 24-hour period beginning with the crossing of the Jordan—it is much more profound than that. Rather he demands that the 'day of decision' of Moab becomes the 'day of response' in Canaan. The transition between the 'days' of 27.1 and 27.2 involves the extension of the 'day of decision' to life on the west bank, in keeping with the dynamic view of 'Moab' described above. We have already suggested that life in the land is to consist of a 'settled nomadism'; in a similar way it is to remain the 'day of decision', even when the fulfilment of promise begins to unfold.[101]

Mt Ebal is thus to become the new Moab, standing in continuity in the land with the succession of places of significance without, and taking its place in the journey of the nation. Anbar was right to see in these verses an attempt to draw together covenantal ideas linked intrinsically to significant places in the life of Israel—but there is also a dynamic progression involved. The new day of decision will be at Ebal—it subsumes the protological choices of Moab, and reiterates yet again the foundational insights of the covenant at Horeb. The journey continues into the land. The command to make the altar draws heavily on Exod. 20.24, and along with the law-stones in v. 8 establishes the relationship between Ebal and Horeb. Thus it seems likely that v. 8 is withheld for rhetorical effect until the identification of Ebal with Horeb through the altar law becomes clear, and then used to make the equation unmistakable.

As the perspective of the preacher shifts increasingly to the future, the significance of Moab recedes, as the frame is filled with the new places of decision awaiting Israel in the land.

The command to sacrifice in 27.7 merits some detailed comment. It is telling that many commentators are virtually silent at this point. It is difficult to ascribe this to a pre-Deuteronomic source which has somehow slipped through the editorial net, as its language and sentiment are so thoroughly Deuteronomic (cf. 12.7, 12, 18 etc.). 'Rejoicing before Yahweh' is a fundamental feature of the altar-law of Deuteronomy 12, which itself is widely regarded as containing the kernel of Deuteronomic theology. If Deuteronomy 12 is regarded as demanding a Jerusalem Cult, then we have run into a major conflict. This potential difficulty disappears if one takes into account the journey motif which is central to the theological outlook of the Deuteronomist. After the conclusion of the lawcode, we move from Moab, the place where Israel is called to

---

101. An interesting comparison to this idea of nomadism in the land comes in Jer. 35, where the Rechabites are described.

decision outside the land, to Ebal. It is hardly surprising that here Israel is called to affirm its allegiance to Yahweh in a cultic setting on entering the land itself. In the light of this spatial dynamic we are not only prepared for but actually *expect* such a radically new expression of the appropriate place to offer sacrifice to Yahweh. Shechem takes its place as one of a succession of significant places in the life of Israel. This is in total agreement with the conclusions of McConville's study of Deuteronomy 12 (see below).

Verses 1-8 therefore provide a fitting response to the lawcode, shifting the focus from Moab to a future place of commitment, another new Horeb, in terms which draw on both the developed temporal and spatial ideas of chs. 1–11 and the altar-law which dominates the code. This exegesis of the text has one further advantage. Deut. 27.9-10 is usually regarded as having little or no connection with either the immediately preceding or succeeding material, but is typically linked instead to 26.16-19. The shift in subject to include the 'levitical priests' is one plank in this argument. But if this passage is concerned to identify Ebal with Horeb, and call Israel to repeat the obedient response of Moab, then it may be that the role of the levitical priests in pronouncing the blessing and curse is part of a complex of events re-enacting the revelation at Horeb and Moab (cf. 18.1-8, the reading of the law in 31.11). The levitical priests are commanded to continue the mediatorial function of Moses.

One striking detail that has occasioned surprisingly little comment is the call to Israel to 'hear' at this point. The resemblance to the Shema is not accidental. I argued above that in context the call to hear is not an empty sapiential technique, but is rather intended to repeat the experience of Horeb in listening to and acting upon the commands of Yahweh. The call to silence is unique in Deuteronomy, which strengthens the injunction even further. The assertion that obedience 'this day' will have definite implications in the future—here specifically the rituals to be enacted on Mt Ebal—serves to bind the past, present and future together in terms of the national experience at Horeb, Moab and Shechem. Once the identification of Shechem as the next significant point of decision in the life of the nation is made, then its significance can be expounded at some length.

## II. *The Levitical Curses (27.11-26)*
This section is not without its problems. In particular the presence of the list of curses, detached from accompanying blessings and unusual in its

demands for obedience (compare the bald condemnations of the curse list of ch. 28), seems to stand in uncomfortable juxtaposition with the surrounding materials. Such a list of curses is unparalleled in the Hebrew Bible.[102]

If Shechem is to replace Moab as the next stage of the rhetorical journey, then one would expect a similar decision to be faced by Israel at Shechem as at Moab. This is exactly the function of this list of curses. As such the list of curses becomes much more readily comprehensible, and moreover an important part of the rhetoric of the chapter.

The other distinctive of the list is found in the prescribed response of Israel *as a whole* to the pronouncement of the Levites. Such a communal response to an announcement of curse is once again unique in the Hebrew Bible.[103] The idea—one nation responding with one voice on entry to the one land—is obviously very much in keeping with Deuteronomic theology of the one people of God (cf. chs. 4 and 5). Along with the demand inherent in each curse for obedience to some element of the revelation at Moab/Horeb (v. 26 subsumes both), it gives this series a radically different character and purpose from the ensuing list of ch. 28.[104] It appears that after the assembling of the twelve tribes

---

102. See W. Schottroff, *Der altisraelitische Fluchspruch* (WMANT, 30; Neukirchen: Neukirchener Verlag, 1969). Schottroff helpfully distinguishes between *Fluchbegründung* and *Fluchbedingung* (p. 74), and comments: 'Die Verbindung des Fluches mit einer *Begründung* zeigt sich vor allem in der Fluchreihe des apodiktischen Rechts Dtn. 27.15-26; dies alles sind *Eventualflüche*', p. 94. Compare S.H. Blank, 'The Curse, Blasphemy, the Spell and the Oath', *HUCA* 23/1 (1950–51), pp. 23-94 (74). Also E. Bellefontaine, 'The Curses of Deut. 27: Their Relationship to the Prohibitives', in *No Famine in the Land* (FS J.L. McKenzie; ed. W. Flanagan and A.W. Robinson; Missoula: Scholars' Press, 1975), pp. 49-61. This article picks up the work of Schulz in *Das Todesrecht im Alten Testament* (BZAW, 114; Berlin: A. Töpelmann, 1969) and argues for an originally corresponding list of blessings based on the same prohibitives. Also I. Lewy, 'The Puzzle of Deut. 27', *VT* 12 (1962), pp. 207-11. Lewy poses several interesting questions regarding the content and vocalizing of the blessings and curses in the light of the command to the Levites in vv. 14-26. Unfortunately his traditio-historical solution is a little far-fetched. See also Alt's discussion of the curses as apodictic law in 'The Origin of Old Testament Law', *Essays on Old Testament History and Religion* (ET; Oxford: Blackwell, 1966), pp. 81-132, and C. Westermann, *Grundformen prophetischer Rede* (BEvT, 31; Munich: Chr. Kaiser Verlag, 1964).

103. Neh 5.13 is an individual parallel.

104. See Schulz, *Das Todesrecht*, p. 61, on this. There are parallels with the Book of the Covenant and the Holiness Code, as well as with earlier parts of Deuteronomy.

on facing peaks, all twelve are to listen to and respond to the annuncia-
tion of these 'legal curses' by the Levites. All Israel is given a stark
reminder of the initiative God has taken in revealing the covenant faithfulness he demands to Israel. The people have no choice but to agree
that this is what God has said, and that his revelation is just. This is a
prerequisite for the graphic illustration of decision to be enacted on
Gerizim and Ebal—before Israel makes the choice to follow Yahweh or
rebel, the content of that very decision, and the origins of the dilemma
facing them, are made abundantly clear. Disobedience after this point
must be culpable, for in the light of vv. 14-26 it must inevitably be
wilful.

The ascription of the words of vv. 14-26 to the Levites is a necessary
development in the establishment of Shechem as the place of decision in
the land. It is quite natural that the Levites (as the guardians of the legal
deposit of the nation) take centre stage, as the people as a whole are
faced with the responsibility which their inheritance brings.[105]

There is clear continuity, then, between the opening verses of this
chapter, the curse list of vv. 14-26, and the Gerizim/Ebal ritual proper.
The purpose of the three separate rituals of ch. 27—inscribing the law
on stones, building an altar, and the levitical rehearsal of 'legal curses'—
is in effect the same: to enable Israel to recapitulate the experiences of
Horeb and Moab at Shechem, enshrining the divine demand for
obedient response in its national consciousness in the land.

### III. *The Blessings and Curses at Gerizim and Ebal (28.1-68)*

The visual impact of events at Shechem was intended to be stunning.
Gerizim was according to Bülow easily the more fertile of the two
mountains.[106] Nowhere would the implications of the decision facing
Israel be more obvious than here. There are several striking features of
the list of curses which are of interest in the context of time and place.[107]

Questions of form and transmission are irrelevant—the important feature is that in the
context of Deut. 27 they inevitably recall earlier revelation.

105. P.C. Craigie, *The Book of Deuteronomy* (NICOT; Grand Rapids:
Eerdmans,1976) notes that only the guardians of the ark pronounce because the rest
of the tribe is positioned on Gerizim, the mountain of blessing.

106. S. Bülow, 'Der Berg des Fluches', *ZDPV* 73 (1957), pp. 100-107.

107. For additional discussions of the curses see D.R. Hillers, *Treaty Curses and
the Old Testament Prophets* (BibOr, 16; Rome: Pontifical Biblical Institute, 1964);
Preuss, *Deuteronomium*, pp. 156-57. For the reasons for and implications of the differences in length and substance of the two series see Millar, *Ethics*.

After the curses take up the specific subject of expulsion from the land in v. 21, the dominant motif becomes a return to Egypt—echoing very strongly the 'Anti-Exodus' theme of the opening chapters. This is introduced explicitly in v. 27, but only Craigie among commentators does justice to any further memory of Egypt underlying the curses. The search for meaning in the treaty parallels may in fact have diverted attention from a much more obvious and theologically significant factor—the reminders of Egypt in the death of livestock (v. 31), anger and anguish under oppression (vv. 32-33), affliction with boils (v. 35), failed harvests due to locusts (v. 38), loss of offspring (v. 41) and reversal of the strata of society (v. 44).[108]

The most compelling piece of evidence comes at the conclusion of this sequence in v. 46. The function of the curses in the life of the nation is to act as a 'sign and a wonder'. This phrase occurred in 4.34, 6.22 and 7.19. In every case it referred to the plagues in Egypt. This is supported by the occurrence of 'signs' in Exod 8.23, 10.1, 2 and 'portents' in 7.3, 11.9, 10.

It is clear that the *function* of this varied list of curses, which draws on much common ancient Near Eastern material, is ultimately to present to Israel in painful detail the consequences of disobedience—this is nothing less than a new journey of reversal, culminating in a renewed exposure to the painful reality of life 'in Egypt' (28.47-48).

This theme is picked up once more at the conclusion of the curses. First in vv. 50-52 the gracious provision enumerated in ch. 8 is systematically withdrawn and overrun. Then the chapter moves to a climax in vv. 59-60. With biting irony it is asserted that the failure of Israel to 'cleave' to Yahweh will result in the plagues of the 'new Egypt' 'cleaving' to Israel.

In a way the proposal to read the entire series of curses from vv. 27-68 as representing a return to Egypt is a rather obvious one. At both ends of the series such an understanding is made explicit, and is in fact demanded by the text. Yahweh's solemn undertaking to bring the nation of Israel back to Egypt in sorrow via the same road they left is a recapitulation of the nation's experience in the wilderness writ large. The journey from Egypt, to Horeb, Moab and eventually Shechem is

---

108. While some of the parallels are supported by vocabulary (e.g. the boils in vv. 27, 35; cf. Exod. 9), this should not exclude other curses (e.g. the locusts) being regarded as referring to the Egypt experience on ground of context and content.

followed by a shocking reversal of an instant return to Egypt direct from Shechem.

We have seen that the list of curses in ch. 29 demonstrates an identical use of the history of Israel to that in chs. 1–3. The historical retrospect set out the journey of Israel in the wilderness post-Kadesh Barnea in terms of an anti-Exodus. The perspective on the future given in ch. 29 is that failure to obey at Shechem in the land itself will result in the same journey back to Egypt. In the future however, the consequences will be much more severe.

Chapters 27 and 28 utilize the same motifs of time and place which dominated chs. 1–11. The correspondence between Horeb and Moab is extended to Shechem. The climactic significance of Moab in the journey of Israel is now extrapolated to Gerizim and Ebal, within the land itself. The future orientation of these closing chapters demands an extension of the same essential concepts which were used parenetically to such effect in the opening phase of the book.

## IV. *The Ratification of the Covenant at Moab (28.69–29.29)*

Much has been made in recent years of the similarities of this section of the text with other ancient covenantal forms.[109] While it is clear that the language and thought of this material has been influenced by contemporary factors, my view is that in this chapter, as elsewhere in the book, ancient forms and conventions have been shaped and reshaped to serve the Deuteronomic agenda. It is therefore the Deuteronomic distinctives which will occupy our attention.

One feature of the chapter which has attracted critical attention for centuries is the reference of 28.69(MT).[110] Some older commentators (including Driver) argued that since the phrase 'the words of the covenant' does not occur after this point in the book, the reference must be to what has gone before. I follow the majority, however, in linking it instead to the following chapter, with its numerous allusions to the covenant.[111]

---

109. See especially K. Baltzer, *The Covenant Formulary* (Oxford: Oxford University Press, 1970), pp. 34ff.; Lohfink, 'Der Bundesschluss im Land Moab: Redaktionsgeschichtliches zu Dt 28,69–32,47', *BZ* (NF), 6 (1962), pp. 32-56.

110. Most EVV make their interpretation explicit by renumbering it as 29.1. See e.g. REB, RSV, NIV, KJV.

111. This is in line with the anticipatory use of 'laws and statutes' highlighted in the discussion of chs. 4 and 5. Even at this advanced stage in the argument of the

It is conventional to treat the 'covenant at Moab' as a discrete section stretching to 30.20, and according to Lohfink all the way to 32.47.[112] There is undoubtedly a coherence of thought running through these chapters, but there are also unmistakable points of transition. The heading at 31.1 is a major obstacle to taking 28.69–32.47 as a formal unity. The continuity shown across major text divisions can be ascribed to coherence in argument and thought, as we have seen throughout the Deuteronomic framework, without having to postulate the existence of extended documents or rigid forms. Irrespective of any covenantal patterns here, we shall consider the section 28.69–30.20 in three separate phases, as seems to be demanded by the rhetoric of the material itself. The first section is 28.69–29.29.

The opening verse of this section, 28.69, is striking for its juxtaposition of Moab and Horeb. Only here is a 'covenant at Moab' explicitly designated, and laid alongside that at Horeb.[113] Preuss argues that in Deuteronomistic thought, Moab replaces Horeb in the light of Israelite disobedience. He is surely correct to highlight the importance of this juxtaposition. But I would suggest that while this unique statement is striking in its expression, its content is the logical culmination of the detailed parallel which has been developed throughout the framework, particularly in chs. 4 and 5. The people at Moab did experience the establishment of the covenant at Horeb within the Deuteronomic view of Israel's corporate history—now they are faced with the upgraded version. The revelation at Moab is presented not as *replacing* Horeb in the life of Israel (*pace* Preuss), but as *augmenting and updating* it for

book, we do not seem to have reached the point where it has all been said.

112. See A. Rofé, 'The Covenant in the Land of Moab Dt 28.69–30.20', in *Das Deuteronomium* (ed. Lohfink), pp. 310-20. Lohfink in 'Der Bundesschluss' states that 'Im Lichte der beiden Überschriften 28,69 und 31,1 bilden diese vier Kapitel eine Einheit. Nach der zugehörigen Überschrift in 28,69 müsste mindestens ein repräsentiver Teil dieses Textblocks "die Worte des Bundes" enthalten den mit den Söhnen Israels im Lande Moab zu schliessen, Jahwe Moses befahl' (p. 35). While his general argument concerning the title in 28.69 holds, he struggles to show that it is necessary to take this whole section as a covenantal text. The similarities he highlights demonstrate continuity of thought, but do not establish the necessity of detecting a covenantal whole.

113. This leads Preuss to comment: 'Hier und nur hier im Alten Testament steht nun Horeb-"Verpflichtung" gegen Moab-"Verpflichtung", d.h. der Dekalog ist die Urkunde des ersteren, das gesamte Dtn. die des zweiten, als Auslegung des Dekalogs, als Entfaltung der Grundgebote' (*Deuteronomium*, p. 158).

the new conditions of life in the land of Canaan. If Israel is to avoid the journey of reversal, then they must abide by the conditions set out at the new Horeb.

It is easy to miss the theological impact of ch. 29 if it is detached from the surrounding material as a covenantal fragment appended to the Deuteronomic parenesis. This integral part of the Deuteronomic scheme sets out the alternatives facing Israel very clearly—life in the land with Yahweh, or the journey back to Egypt. Israel's future will be determined by the response made to the initiatives of Yahweh today at Moab and tomorrow at Shechem, in the light of yesterday at Horeb.

The fundamental continuity of the national experience of covenant is made explicit in 29.1-3. As in chs. 1–11, the whole nation is addressed as if every member had been present at every stage in its history, including suffering the oppression of Egypt. The same is true of the idealistic representation of the wilderness years (cf. 8.4), the conquest of Sihon and Og, and the occupation of Transjordan. This presentation of the journey of Israel is in effect a selective account of the opening three chapters, and it culminates in v. 8 in an injunction to adhere to the stipulations of this covenant.

Verses 9-14 expand on the central theme of response to the covenant, which is presented as the same covenant made with Israel at Horeb. The language throughout is that of reiteration or renewal rather than replacement.[114] The covenant at Moab is also presented as a fulfilment of the promise to Abram in Genesis 15 (where the same use of עבר occurs). This is consistent with the declaration of Exod. 19.5 that Yahweh will be Israel's God and they will be his people (cf. 26.16-19, 28.9 etc.). Moab gathers up all of Israel's pre-history in a climactic moment of decision which subsumes all that has gone before. Learning to live at this moment—first at Shechem and then throughout the land—will be the key to a successful occupation and ongoing life with Yahweh in the land. Verse 14 ties this 'covenant' with every earlier expression of Yahweh's commitment to Israel, and demands an identical response. The timeless element is the key—the ultimate significance for Israel is not to be sought in a once-for-all ritual, based on common

---

114. See Miller, *Deuteronomy*, p. 200: 'The chief clues for understanding this second covenant are found in recognising the boundary character of Deuteronomy, the place of this covenant in the structure of the book, and Deuteronomy's concern for actualizing in the present moment the relationship between God and Israel and the demands and consequences of that relationship'.

covenantal patterns, but in the whole-hearted ethical response demanded of them today and for all time to come. This chapter is concerned above all with theology, not ritual.

The consequences of each individual failing to take the obligation to obey Yahweh seriously are considered in the rest of this passage (15.15-28).

At several crucial points the journey motif recurs. In v. 15 the whole argument is rooted in the experience of travelling from Egypt 'through the nations' in terms which are unmistakably echoes of chs. 1–3. In marked contrast the nations are depicted as coming to witness the desolation in Israel (v. 21), which in turn is compared to the destruction of Sodom, Gomorrah, Admah and Zeboiim. Instead of the nations' declaration of Israel's derivative superiority in 4.5-8, we now see them asking for an explanation of Yahweh's punishment of his own people.

Nothing is spared in the drive to push Israel towards loving obedience. In ch. 28 it is the threat of a journey back to Egypt for the people of God which must motivate them to obey. In ch. 29 Israel must reckon with the tragedy and humiliation of the nations making a journey to the land of Israel, to witness the disastrous effects of Yahweh's righteous anger with that same people.

## V. *After the Curse—Return from 'Egypt' (30.1-10)*

There is such a distinct change of mood at 30.1 that it is difficult to see how it can be regarded as of one cultic or covenantal piece with what has gone before. Rofé describes it as 'a majestic fugue on the theme of שוב'. [115]

The major theme of the preceding chapters has been the possibility under the curse of the journey of reversal, the anti-Exodus to an unimaginable situation in a new 'Egypt'. Chapter 30 reasserts the grace of Yahweh, and the amazing possibility of that journey of reversal once more being itself 'reversed'. It is in this context of the journey of Israel that the full force of the possibility of return can be grasped. In Deuteronomic theology, repentance (viz. return to Yahweh) and return (to the land) are inextricably linked. This is a further dimension of the journey theology of the book. The life of Israel is consistently presented, from Egypt to Canaan, and now in the distant future, as a journey which may be reversed, and then by the grace of Yahweh resumed.

This section also sees the emergence of 'new covenant' thought,

115. 'Covenant', p. 311.

usually associated with Jeremiah or Ezekiel, in Deut. 30.6-10. Initially repentance issues in the expected return to the land for Israel (vv. 4-5). Then, echoing the command of Yahweh in 10.16 to 'Circumcise your hearts', we find an new element—the expectation of an eschatological circumcision, enabling the fulfilment of the kernel of the Deuteronomic prescriptions.[116] In the face of the disobedience of the past, spelled out with such care, the acknowledgement of the acute need for divine intervention in the life of the individual is a natural, though striking, progression.

The terms of the reversal of fortunes experienced by Israel as a result of this repentance and the radical intervention of Yahweh are couched in familiar terms—the curses will be turned on the enemies of Yahweh and Israel, who will once more enjoy his neo-paradisal benefits. Both the elements of Israel's repentance (vv. 1-2, 9-10) and Yahweh's intervention ( vv. 4-6) are essential to the thought of the chapter, and are cast in terms of the journey of Israel.

There is a double movement in the chapter encapsulated in the word שׁוב. Initially the move is made by Israel as they return to Yahweh, pledging their allegiance to him afresh in their landless, scattered situation. The concomitant physical motion is the convergence of the exiles once more to the land which Yahweh promised to them.

The play on שׁוב in these verses has two effects. First it establishes the final phase in the journey of Israel as expulsion from the land and scattering throughout the nations, and a final eschatological return.[117] In addition to this it reiterates that the primary journey undertaken by Israel is not concerned simply with geographical factors—it is ultimately a spiritual journey, the progress of which is determined solely by obedient response to Yahweh.

## VI. *The Climax of the Deuteronomic Parenesis (30.11-20)*

This section provides a powerful climax to the rhetoric of the book. Nowhere is the choice facing Israel so starkly presented. As Lohfink

---

116. This new covenant perspective inevitably sets up a tension with the statements in 30.11-20 which present Israel as being capable of obeying the Deuteronomic law *without* this radical solution of divine circumcision of the heart. This is part of the Deuteronomic perspective on obedience which seems at once to be within reach and unreachable; see Millar, 'Ethics'.

117. The descriptions of the situation on return to the land exceed anything which has occurred earlier in the book.

states, vv. 11-14 is a discrete unit, paving the way for the parenesis of vv. 15-20.[118] In it, in contrast to the assertion of the need for Yahweh to circumcise the hearts of Israel, it is made plain that Israel has the wherewithal to respond positively to the covenantal demands of Yahweh. The use of 'this commandment' suggests that the reference is to the content of Deuteronomy in general, as we have seen elsewhere.[119] Verse 14 is fascinating—in language reminiscent of 6.6, 11.18 and most strikingly 4.5-8, it is declared that this דבר, like God himself, is very near: on their lips and even in their hearts. The inference is that Israel are in the perfect position to respond in obedience to Yahweh's words.[120] The only thing which can prevent them from deciding to go the way of the Lord is wanton disobedience. This sums up the challenge of chs. 27–29.

The final six verses gather up almost all of the ideas which have been developed in the course of the book in appealing to Israel to obey Yahweh. The decision facing Israel, which has been the controlling concept in so much of what has been written, is reduced to its most potent form—it is a choice between life and death, good and evil. This most fundamental of choices must be faced today at Moab, tomorrow at Shechem and every day of life in the land. Verses 16-18 again summarize the content of the blessing/curse material in chs. 27–29, as a premature end to the journey is graphically portrayed. In the covenantal language of v. 19 the basic decision is reiterated, with the added dimension of the significance of today's choice for the generations of tomorrow. This future motivation is finally joined with the past, as the final appeal is made to the Patriarchal traditions in the stereotyped Deuteronomic language with which we have become so familiar.

It is well established that ch. 30 is moving in the same thought-world as ch. 4. The briefest glance at 30.1-3 and 4.29-31 is enough to confirm that. We described ch. 4 as an overture to the rest of the book. Chapter 30 is linked to ch. 4, but only as the finale is linked to the overture—in ch. 30 the themes introduced in ch. 4 reach their *dénouement*. These two chapters can be regarded as an *inclusio* for the rhetorical structure

---

118. 'Der Bundesschluss', p. 42.

119. See the discussion of Braulik's 'Die Ausdrücke für Gesetz' in relation to ch. 4.

120. The contrast with v. 6 is probably to be understood in terms of the quality of their obedience. Ultimately divine action is necessary for the consistent fulfilment of the spirit and letter of the law. In the immediate present Israel is equipped to 'choose to serve Yahweh'.

of the book as a whole. But they do not stand apart from it. Only chs. 4 and 30 can give meaning to the intervening material, and the true connection between the overture and finale can only be seen in the light of the completed work.

There is a very real sense in which the zenith of the exhortation of the book is reached here. It is as if nothing more can be said. If the people of Israel have not been moved to obey by now, then they will not be moved. Yet there remains one major matter to be cleared up—the death of Moses. I take chs. 31–34 to be a postscript, exhibiting many of the parenetic features of what has gone before, yet dealing essentially with only one thing—the death of Moses and the progress of the people to Canaan under new leadership. There is sufficient continuity to demand that they are regarded as an inherent part of Deuteronomy, yet the theological concerns here seem to broaden to encompass new themes in keeping with a different point of transition in the life of Israel, as Moses hands on the torch to Joshua.

### The Appendix: Chapters 31–34

There has been little interest paid to the theology of these chapters. Especially since Noth, they have been assigned, due to their similarity to chs. 1–3, to the Deuteronomistic version of the history of Israel, and most critical energy has been devoted to answering questions of form and source. Since, however, we have seen good reason to question the assignment of chs. 1–3 to DtH, this should not be taken for granted.

I would propose that the closing chapters of the book are in fact a postscript to chs. 1–30. They undoubtedly come after the climax of the parenesis, but that does not mean that all that follows is simply to be dismissed. This material is intensely relevant to the rest of Deuteronomy. These four chapters deal with outstanding matters in the life of Moses and Israel, and in doing so give further examples of the basic theological perspective which our study of the rest of the framework has revealed.

### I. *The Succession of Joshua (31.1-8)*

The postscript to the Deuteronomic parenesis begins with the matter of a successor for Moses. For our purposes it is interesting to note that the central motif of 31.2-8 is exactly that which we find in chs. 1–3. The motivation for Israelite acceptance of the appointment of Joshua to lead them is that, with him, the journey of Israel will continue to enjoy the success stemming from the presence of Yahweh in their midst. The idea that this presence controls Israel's advance is so dominant that the mention of Joshua in v. 3b almost comes as an afterthought. It is not surprising that Joshua's personal commission is couched in similar terms.

It is interesting that Lohfink comments that in this section we are on the frontier between the Mosaic speeches and the Deuteronomistic narrative, beginning with Joshua.[121] It is inevitable that in this final movement of the Mosaic corpus concerns other than those we have observed in the main Deuteronomic corpus must be taken into account. We are at one of the major transition points in the history of Israel, as the work of Moses draws to a close. This undoubtedly has influenced both the purpose and presentation of this material. The death of a leader such as Moses cannot be quickly and quietly passed over, especially when in itself it underlines the message of obedience which has been preached so powerfully in the rest of Deuteronomy.

## II. *Writing and Reading the Law (31.9-13)*
Moses' instruction to write down the law and read it to the nation *en masse* at regular intervals coheres neatly with much of what we have seen. It supports the repeated injunctions to remember what Yahweh has done and what Israel has learned at every stage of her journey, and in turn the accompanying necessity that Israel re-enact the decisions at Horeb, Moab and Shechem at each and every moment of their national existence.

The fact that the significance of this ritual is not spelled out in more detail may suggest that the primary concern of this portion of the book is not parenetic. Instead we have here the last testament of Moses—his final injunctions need no further elaboration. This is a recurrent feature of chs. 31–34. The preoccupation seems to be presenting the words of the dying leader rather than offering comment on them.[122]

## III. *Moses' Swan Song (31.14–32.44)*
The concern to record rather than preach seems also to be paramount in the remainder of chs. 31 and 32. Yahweh's final words to Moses return to the issue which raised its head briefly in ch. 30: can Israel obey, and

---

121. See also Lohfink, 'Die deuteronomische Darstellung des Übergangs der Führung Israels von Moses auf Josue', in *Studien*, pp. 83-97. Originally *Scholastik* 37 (1962), pp. 32-44.

122. This is a problem for those wanting to see these chapters as part of a Deuteronomistic composition.

are they prepared to? Yahweh, in the most striking revelation of the future in the whole book, makes it clear to Moses that Israel will experience blessing and curse in turn, because ultimately their stubborn nature will prevail (cf. 30.6). The provision of the Song (and the Book as a whole—v. 24) is to point the nation back to Yahweh in its time of rebellion.

Much has been written about the Song of Moses but it seems fair to say that discussion has centred on the form of the Song, and the influences which were responsible for its shape and tone, rather than on the content *per se*.[123] Wright and Baumann argued that the form of the chapter is an example of the so-called 'ריב pattern', a divine lawsuit, a position most recently defended by Mayes.[124] While this seems to have attained a degree of acceptance, in any case it is advisable to note that, as with treaty structures in general, we do not have a slavish imitation of a fixed form. Thompson helpfully observes that the Song 'is not strictly a covenant law-suit document, but a didactic document based on covenant law-suit pictures'.[125] Other studies have tried to root the song in a wisdom milieu, or to use linguistic methods to determine the origin of the poem, but it would be fair to say that study of the chapter is still characterized by a degree of agnosticism.[126]

The search for a *Sitz im Leben* is also extremely problematical. The Song does not refer to specific historical events, and is couched in (deliberately?) vague terms. There is nothing in its content that excludes it from being exactly what it claims to be—a hymnic composition from

123. Preuss, *Deuteronomium*, 166-8.

124. G.E. Wright, 'The Lawsuit of God', in *Israel's Prophetic Heritage* (FS J. Muilenburg; ed. B.W. Anderson and W. Harrelson; London: SCM Press, 1962), pp. 26-67; E. Baumann, 'Das Lied Moses auf seine gedankliche Geschlossenheit untersucht', *VT* 6 (1956), pp. 414-24. Mayes, *Deuteronomy*, has a succinct summary of the arguments, with the OT parallels on pp. 380-81. Mendenhall contests any such form with great vigour in 'Samuel's Broken *Rîb*: Deut. 32', in *No Famine in the Land* (FS J.L. McKenzie; ed. W. Flanegan and A.W. Robinson; Missoula: Scholars Press, 1975).

125. J.A. Thompson, *Deuteronomy* (TOTC; Leicester: IVP, 1974), p. 297.

126. For wisdom theories see particularly J.R. Boston, 'Wisdom Influence', pp. 166-78; also von Rad, *Deuteronomy*. Linguistic studies by O. Eissfeldt, *Das Lied Moses* (Berichte über die Verhandlung der Sächsischen Akademie der Wissenschaften zu Leipzig, 104/5, 1958); W.F. Albright, 'Some Remarks', pp. 339-46; also D.A. Robertson, *Linguistic Evidence in Dating Early Hebrew Poetry*, (SBLDS, 3; Missoula: Scholars Press, 1972).

the very earliest national traditions of Israel on the verge of the land, as Moses looks rather pessimistically to the immediate future and beyond to the hope of eventual restoration.

It is important to notice that the theological material in the Song does cohere well with the overall themes of Deuteronomy. Ultimately we cannot be certain about the origins of this piece, nor of the way the Deuteronomist may or may not have adapted material to serve his purpose. What is clear is that it is not an unthinking addition to the text, nor simply an ancient pericope preserved purely for historiographic purposes, but rather an important part of the movement of the ethical agenda of Deuteronomy to its final climax as the day of Moses draws to a close.

The main thrust of the Song appeals to Israel to come back to the point of decision, to reverse the direction of its journey in a time of apostasy. Verses 10-14 are a poetic representation of the progress of Israel from Egypt through the Wilderness to the land. Their failure to learn from this journey leads them to fall foul of the dangers spelled out in ch. 8, and they are exposed to the wrath of Yahweh. Lohfink has rightly observed that there is an axis in 32.26-27 about which the whole Song revolves. The first half of the Song deals with the failure of Israel to live a life of covenant faithfulness in the distant and recent past, and the resultant curses with which Yahweh smites them. But v. 26 admits the possibility of a return to blessing because Yahweh is still essentially for his people, and v. 29 opens the door to restoration via repentance.

The Song of Moses is not the most complete expression of Deuteronomic thought. Its central message, however, although couched in poetic form, remains that there is a decision facing Israel in the present and the future which will determine the very nature (and setting) of its national life. In this it is in complete sympathy with the framework of the book.

## IV. *The Death of Moses (32.45–34.12)*

The last, ominous words of Moses to Israel (32.45-47) pick up the theme of 30.15-20, urging Israel to obey at any cost. The closing words of the blessing (33.26-29) depict Israel finally settled in the land, secure and obedient because of covenant faithfulness. This eschatological consummation for Israel is followed by the narration of the death of the great leader.

Coats has subjected the account of his death to a detailed literary study, concluding that an original heroic ending, to be compared to that of other ancient mythical figures, has been subjected to a late rationalization to account for Moses' failure to enter the land.[127] His study, however, is not compelling. The exclusion of Moses from the land is a dark theme which runs through the whole book, serving to adumbrate the consequences of disobedience for the people in the most powerful way.

Such has been the importance of the theme of place in general, and of Moab in particular, that the death of Moses itself at an unknown spot in Moab cannot be completely divested of exemplary significance. Moses dies at the point of decision, because of past failure. Israel, under its new leader, is left to make the decision on its own, aware of the fate of the man who knew Yahweh intimately. Even the death of Moses provides further impetus to the call for Israel to obey.

*Conclusion*
The final part of the framework of Deuteronomy falls broadly into two sections. The first (chs. 27–30) draws on the identification of Moab with Horeb as places of decision in the opening chapters of the book (see 28.69), and extends the idea of the covenantal journey of Israel to Shechem within the land itself. The place of decision in the present holds the key for safe negotiation for the succession of places of decision, beginning with Shechem, in the future. The consequences of this decision are portrayed in terms of the journey from (and back towards) Egypt, in an identical way to chs. 1–3. Chapter 30, along with ch. 4, forms an *inclusio* for the main thrust of the Deuteronomic parenesis, showing that the covenant journey is perpetual, and can only be successfully negotiated by obedient response to the law of God revealed at Horeb and Moab, and reiterated in the land.

The book is brought to a close with a historical postscript, focusing on the final words and death of Moses. As the book began with a historical example enshrining its theological message, so it closes. The death of Moses outside the land at the place of decision sounds a solemn warning to the nation of the consequences of disobedience. The Mosaic era closes on an ominous note. Thus distinctive Deuteronomic concerns are visible right to the end always pushing Israel on to obedience in response to the grace of Yahweh. In every place and at all times, Israel's primary responsibility is to live in covenant faithfulness to Yahweh, deciding to love him and live for him alone.

127. G.W. Coats, 'Legendary Elements in the Moses Death Reports', *CBQ* 39 (1977), pp. 34-44.

### Conclusions: Time and Place in the Framework of Deuteronomy

The framework of Deuteronomy is dominated by the journey of Israel
through a succession of national crises. At each point, the people of God
face a decision. That decision remains essentially the same—to respond
to the love of Yahweh shown to them by loving him in return. This love
is to be expressed in obedience to his revealed word.

In Egypt obedience consisted simply of getting up and setting out on
this journey. At Horeb the terms of the covenant relationship were first
expounded. At Kadesh the fulfilment of promise hinged on taking
Yahweh the warrior at his word. Now, at Moab, the lessons of Israelite
history as a whole are used to encourage Israel to go forward, and to
take a fresh, radical decision to submit to the word of Yahweh—now
applied at length to life in Canaan in the preaching of Moses. But even
then the journey is not over. Successful occupation of the land depends
on the decisions of Israel in the future. Wrong decisions will inevitably
lead to loss of the land. But even beyond that eventuality, Israel is called
in the future to decide once more to submit to the divine command, this
time in repentance.

It is through this rhetorical scheme of journey through time and place
that Deuteronomy addresses some of its major themes. In particular, the
evolution of the Deuteronomic concept of law is embedded deeply in
this journey. The historical retrospect of chs. 1–3, the overture of ch. 4
with its profound ideas of corporate nationhood, transcendence and
immanence, the Decalogue and sustained exhortation of chs. 5–11 are all
essential to this process, and crucial if the Lawcode is to be understood
in its proper context. Chapters 27–30 contain some of the most
powerful preaching in the book, and along with the pointed postscript of
Moses' Death at the boundary of the land in chs. 31–34, complete the
picture. History for Israel cannot be separated from covenant faithfulness. Success cannot be achieved without it. Yesterday, Today and
Tomorrow, wherever the nation finds itself—in the land or outside it—a
simple decision faces Israel: to live for Yahweh or not—to move further
into the land with Yahweh, or to go back to Egypt. There can be no
standing still.

# TIME, PLACE AND THE DEUTERONOMIC ALTAR-LAW

## J.G. McConville

### Introduction

The aim of the following essay is to examine Deuteronomy's law regarding the place of worship, variously known as the altar-law, or centralization-law (Deut. 12.5 etc.), in the context of the theology of the book as a whole. It needs little demonstration that this law is of great significance in Deuteronomy. It dominates the so-called law-code (Deut. 12–26), in which worship is a major theme, appearing not only in laws that concern worship directly (Deut. 12; 14.22-29; 15.19-23; 16.1-17, 21; 18.1-8; 26.1-15), but also in a law about administration of justice (17.8-13). It also occurs in one worship context outside the law-code (31.11). There is a certain constancy of form, so that one may speak with some justice of a 'formula', yet, as has often been noticed, this is by no means rigid. Its longest form occurs at Deut. 12.5 ('But you shall seek the place that the LORD your God will choose out of all your tribes as his habitation to put his name there', NRSV). Shorter forms, different from each other, occur in the same chapter at vv. 11, 14, 18, 21. Nevertheless, the formula is recognizable wherever it occurs by the idea of the LORD's choice of a place (מקום) of worship, which remains unnamed. Its special association with him is often expressed in terms of his 'name'. This feature is part of the controversy with other gods implied in the formula; the 'place' is to be Israel's place of worship as Yahweh is to be its God.

Since the formula occurs recognizably, and is distributed over a large section of the book, there is a *prima facie* case for a synchronic study of it. (G. Millar's study has in effect begun to do this). The exercise seems to be worth undertaking because it is rarely attempted. In modern interpretation, the altar-law is generally evaluated in the context of a literary- and historical-critical approach to Deuteronomy, which takes Josiah's reform as its principal point of reference, and seeks to penetrate the layers of literary and theological accretion in the book (sometimes with the help of the slight variations of the formula itself).

In my view this approach militates against a proper appreciation of the part which the law plays in creating the resonances of a book whose complexities lie more in its thought than has been widely understood. It also makes questionable assumptions about the orientation of Deuteronomy to the reform, when it assumes that the former is a programme for the latter, that is, a document intended to bolster a politico-religious establishment. There are, therefore, both theological and historical-critical aspects of our study, as well as literary ones. These aspects, indeed, are the primary concern of the present study. Conventional methodologies have obscured, I believe, the theologically and politically radical character of Deuteronomy.

The crucial part of the study, however, will be an examination of the altar-law in relation to certain motifs which are fundamentally important in Deuteronomy, principally those of time and place. This exercise will culminate in a comparison of Deuteronomy 12 with Deuteronomy 4. Before coming to that argument, however, we shall consider the way in which Deuteronomy's altar-law has been understood in its later history, from ancient times till the present, to see whether there are common features in a range of disparate interpretations. We will then be in a position to undertake a literary and theological evaluation of the law.

## 1. *Interpretation of the Altar-Law in Historical Perspective*

### *The Old Testament*

A survey of the interpretation of the altar-law begins inevitably in the Old Testament itself. It is not straightforward, of course, to trace that interpretation, because to do so raises certain literary-critical questions. Precisely what Old Testament literature may be said to interpret the altar-law? There is, of course, a body of material for which the answer is straightforward, that is, texts which actually use the formula, or variations of it. There may, however, be other texts which react to the theology of the altar-law in ways which are not immediately obvious. The identification of these requires literary-critical judgments to be made. For example, it has often been held that the law of the altar in Leviticus 17 (H) is a critical response to that of Deuteronomy, repudiating the permissive exceptions which the latter allows in respect of the non-sacrificial slaughter of animals for food.[1] Consideration of this

---

1.    See M. Noth, *Leviticus* (London: SCM Press, 1965), p. 130.

kind of issue is best left, on balance, until the discussion below of modern interpretations of the altar-law, especially of the relationship between Deuteronomy and 'P'.

## DtH and Jeremiah

We consider first, then, passages which refer explicitly to the law. Many of these occur, not surprisingly, in Deuteronomic or related literature. The question as to the identity of the place may seem to be settled by allusions in 1 Kgs 8.29; 2 Kgs 21.4, where it is named as Jerusalem. It is clear that DtH sees the arrival of the Ark of the Covenant in Jerusalem under the aegis of King David as in some sense a culmination of the story of Israel which begins on the plains of Moab and tells of the conflicts, internal and external, which are resolved in the peace which David's victories bring to Israel. The narrative of David's establishment of both himself and the Ark in Jerusalem looks back to Deuteronomy 12 (2 Sam. 7.1, cf. Deut. 12.9), and presumably the events recorded of Jerusalem are told in the light of Deuteronomy's concept of a place which the LORD would choose for his worship.

The question of the altar-law's intention, however, is not completely answered by these observations. DtH actually reflects the law with some suppleness in its developing narrative. A first allusion occurs in the story of Joshua's subjugation of the Gibeonites as sanctuary-servants, in a way that is consonant with the altar-law's own refusal to identify a particular place (Josh. 9.27).

Identification begins in Joshua, however, with the sanctuary at Shiloh, with clear Deuteronomic motifs appearing in the important passage Josh. 18.1-10. These include the land as an inheritance, the Levites' lack of a territorial inheritance, and the allocation of land in Transjordan to Gad, Reuben and the half-tribe of Manasseh. It is the phrase 'before the LORD' twice in vv. 8-10 that establishes a link between this passage and Deuteronomy 12, identifying Shiloh as the place in question. The idea of the chosen place is then predominantly evoked by Shiloh from Joshua to Samuel (cf. Judg. 21.19; 1 Sam. 1.9).

Shiloh is not the only place which evokes the formula, however. Israel worships 'before the LORD' at Bethel also, in a passage which states that the Ark of the LORD stood there 'in those days'. It seems, indeed, that in DtH it is the presence of the Ark that is really important in the unfolding story of Israel's worship. This remains true when David establishes Jerusalem (2 Sam. 6.14).

The interpretation of DtH with regard to the altar-law needs careful consideration, therefore. While it is true that 2 Samuel 7 associates the city with the Deuteronomic passage concerning the altar-law, it is not clear that the narrative of the bringing of the Ark to Jerusalem is a definitive fulfilment of the law. That same narrative is not unambiguous in relation to Jerusalem and the temple-project, and claims for the LORD a certain detachment from the permanency implied by David's plan. Furthermore, the end of the narrative of DtH, in a more literal sense, is the Babylonian exile, a fact which puts the rapturous account of Josiah's reform in a more sober light. DtH certainly does not assert in any straightforward way that the law is fulfilled in the Jerusalem temple. In fact, its story might be said to point up the problematical nature of the establishment of a permanent cult.

The relation of DtH to the altar-law, therefore, should be considered on a broad canvas. While Jerusalem is explicitly named in allusions to the law, other places are also clearly brought into association with it. The story of DtH, in the end, is of a covenant that has been broken chronically throughout a history which has moved through several stages. The idea that the monarchic stage of the story is the crucial one—and therefore that Deuteronomy's law is but a veiled reference to Jerusalem—is not self-evident, and belongs with a particular view of the composition and purpose of both Deuteronomy and DtH. We shall return to this point. A reading of DtH, therefore, leaves the question open as to the intention of the altar-law itself.

A further important consideration comes from Jer. 7.12, which applies the altar-law to Shiloh. In this it shows that it has reflected on both the formula and on the subsequent story in DtH. Jeremiah, furthermore, lies close in certain respects to DtH (whether or not it is regarded as in the strict sense 'Deuteronomistic').[2] In the immediate context of our passage, the phrase המקום הזה (Jer. 7.3, 6, 7), and perhaps elsewhere, is part of the same cast of thought as the Deuteronomic language about the altar (cf. Jer. 19.3-9; Zeph. 1.4; cf. also 2 Kgs 22.16-20). The importance of the Jeremiah passage, however, lies not only in its obvious Deuteronomic echoes, but also in its sense in context (Jer. 7.1-15). Its meaning is precisely that the altar-law could not be fulfilled in the

---

2.    I have argued elsewhere that the book of Jeremiah is not a Deuteronomistic product in the strict sense: *Judgment and Promise: An Interpretation of the Book of Jeremiah* (Leicester: Apollos; Winona Lake: Eisenbrauns, 1993). It is clear, however, that it has certain features in common with DtH.

thoughtless liturgy of the Jerusalem temple or of any other place. If Shiloh could at one time have been 'the chosen place' and yet have been destroyed by Yahweh, then what is asserted is Yahweh's freedom over times and places (not, incidentally, a coolness to cultic religion as such). The Jeremiah passage appears to have reflected on the narrative of DtH and understood it in this way. Such an understanding was by no means foreign either, I have suggested, to that narrative. And in this respect both DtH and Jeremiah are in the spirit of the altar-law itself, which named no place and stressed the choice of Yahweh.[3]

## The Psalms

Clear allusions to the altar-law in other parts of the Old Testament are relatively few. The Psalms suggest two considerations, the first concerning Zion theology. The relationship between Deuteronomy and Zion theology is complex. Whether certain Psalms contain allusions to the altar-law is unclear. Psalm 132 certainly has echoes of Deuteronomy 12 in language and thought (especially vv. 5-8, 13-14), and also stands close to the perspective on the Deuteronomic tradition in 2 Samuel 7 (Ps. 132.11-12). Commentators debate whether the Psalm is strictly Deuteronomic or whether it has other antecedents.[4] It does not, in any case, provide the only perspective on Deuteronomy in the Book of Psalms. Psalm 78 has another. While it does apply the idea of choice of a sanctuary to Zion (v. 68), it also reflects, in its rehearsal of Israel's earliest history, not Deuteronomy alone but the broader perspective on the chosen place which we have seen in DtH. It does this by acknowledging Shiloh as the place where Yahweh first made his dwelling (Ps. 78.60; interestingly, in making the allusion, it uses the verb שׁכן also found in Deut. 12.5). The abrupt ending of the Psalm leaves open the question whether it intends to affirm that Jerusalem, and nowhere else, is the chosen place, or whether, as in Jeremiah 7, the allusion to Shiloh is intended to hang menacingly over Jerusalem and the covenant people.

---

3.    I disagree therefore with D.R. Jones, who thinks that Jeremiah is 'subtly and substantially different' from Deuteronomy in its view of the temple (*Jeremiah* [London: Marshall Pickering, 1992], pp. 143-44). While he is correct in his interpretation of Jeremiah's 'temple sermon', I question his view that Deuteronomy promotes the idea of God dwelling in the Jerusalem temple. This is the view which I am concerned to challenge in the present study.

4.    See L. Allen, *Psalms 101–150* (Waco, TX: Word, 1983), pp. 139-41.

The second consideration relates to the Book of Psalms' reflection on the Zion tradition. It is obvious that a number of Psalms celebrate Jerusalem as the place where God dwells (e.g. Pss. 48, 76). It could hardly be otherwise during the existence of Solomon's temple. This, however, is not the whole story. Rather, the Psalms are part of a tradition which had in time to reckon with the loss of the temple, as the present book of Psalms shows (e.g. Pss. 74, 89). The Zion tradition as such in the Psalms is problematical therefore. Where that tradition has interacted expressly with the Deuteronomic, furthermore, it does not suggest (or certainly not always) a triumphalist interpretation of the latter in favour of Jerusalem (Ps. 78, 89—the latter because of vv. 38-52).

### Other Parts of the Old Testament

In the case of the eighth-century prophets, the question of their relation to Deuteronomic language and ideas is as complex as in the case of the Psalms, though some see proto-Deuteronomic thought there.[5] The books associated with them, of course, are widely held to have undergone Deuteronomistic editing, and therefore in principle one is justified in looking for clear allusions to the altar-law there. However, not even the Zion-orientation of the Book of Isaiah throws up an express allusion, though there may be hints at Isa. 18.7; 66.1. Other 'Zion' statements in the eighth-century prophets may simply sit within a general Zion tradition (e.g. Amos 1.2), yet hardly in a triumphalist way (cf. Amos 6.1).[6] On the other hand, Micah's stern warning (3.9-12) was congenial to the view of Jeremiah which we have noticed above (cf. Jer. 26.17-18).

Where traces of the altar-law may be found in the prophets, therefore, the understanding of it is naturally dominated, as in the Psalms, by the fact of the temple in Jerusalem. However, the strain of prophetic critique prevents the law from being understood as an instrument of a politico-religious *status quo*.

Apart from DtH and Jeremiah, the only other clear allusions to the law are found in the Chronistic literature. Some of this simply takes over expressions already in the Books of Kings (e.g. 2 Chron. 7.12; 33.4; 34.24-28). This is significant in itself, however, as a reaffirmation in the

---

5.   See E.W. Nicholson, *God and his People* (Oxford: Clarendon, 1986), p. 187.

6.   F.I. Andersen and D.N. Freedman think that the 'Zion'-perspective in Amos embraces both a prophetic critique of the whole nation, north and south, and an expectation of an ultimate renewal of the Davidic empire (*Amos* [AB; New York: Doubleday, 1989], pp. 223-24; 898-905).

Second Temple period of the understanding that the altar-law finds fulfilment in Jerusalem. This interpretation of the formula in the Chronistic
literature is further evidenced by Neh. 1.9. It cannot be assumed,
however, as it once was, that 'restorationist' literature of this sort sees
the return from exile as an 'end' of God's history with the covenant
people.[7]

Obviously, the post-exilic literature contains more broadly based
discourse about 'Zion' than the mere appropriation of Deuteronomy's
altar-law. Zion theology is expressed in various ways by Deutero-Isaiah,
Ezekiel, Haggai and Zechariah. On the other hand, signs of dissent have
been found in Isaiah 56-66.[8] And the Books of Daniel and Esther, in different ways, shift the focus of Judaism from temple and land to
Diaspora.[9] In this context, the Deuteronomic formula finds its home
most naturally in literature which, with the caveat entered above, may
be called 'restorationist'.

A survey of clear Old Testament allusions to the altar-law finds that it
is generally understood in relation to Jerusalem. This is not surprising, as
the literature in question emanates from the period after the building of
Solomon's temple, and in the case of Chronicles and Nehemiah, in the
Second Temple period. Application of the altar-law, however, had to be
distinguished from the Zion tradition as such. Clear allusions to it,
furthermore, did not unambiguously see its 'fulfilment' in Jerusalem as
the culmination of the story of Israel and worship. Many of them are in
contexts which proclaim, or hint at, judgment. This is true especially of
Jeremiah and Kings. Where these look beyond the judgment, they do
not agree on the role of Jerusalem; Jeremiah pictures a return to the city,
while Kings is silent on the matter.[10]

The application of the altar-law to Shiloh in Jer. 7.12 and Ps. 78.60
is the most interesting outcome of this survey. The possibility of

7.    See H.G.M. Williamson, 'Eschatology in Chronicles', *TB* 28 (1977),
pp. 115-54; Williamson, *Ezra, Nehemiah* (Waco, TX: Word,1985), p. li.

8.    See P.D. Hanson, *The Dawn of Apocalyptic* (Philadelphia: Fortress Press,
1979), pp. 79-208. Hanson's particular thesis is open to question, but passages such
as Isa. 57, 63.15-19 seem to put in doubt the promises of restoration found in
Isa. 40–55.

9.    See especially S.B. Berg, *The Book of Esther: Motifs, Themes and Structures*
(Missoula: Scholars Press, 1979).

10.   See my '1 Kings viii 46-53 and the Deuteronomic Hope', *VT* 42 (1992),
pp. 67-79.

interpretations of this sort, in the Old Testament literature itself, shows that the altar-law cannot be supposed to have 'intended' to identify the chosen place as Jerusalem. Where such an identification is made, it follows from the setting and purpose of the literature in question. Even then, such literature does not necessarily see the 'choice' of Zion/Jerusalem as the end of God's story with Israel. On the contrary, it is arguable that Zion, far from being an end-point, or dénouement, of the Old Testament story, is rather posed as a problem that still awaits a solution.[11] That problem arises sharply from the tension between, on the one hand, the 'givenness' of city and temple—a givenness implied in the symbolism of the temple itself, and perhaps of the city as political capital, and on the other, the liability of an errant covenant people to judgment. Such a tension is clearest in the prophets, but is found elsewhere also, including the Deuteronomic and related literature.

### Ancient Jewish Interpretation

When we turn to consider the understanding of the altar-law in ancient Jewish interpretation, some of the same caveats apply as in the case of the Old Testament. In the post-biblical period, Jerusalem and the temple remained, in general, the centre of Jewish religion. Much of the literature of the period reflects this. The Wisdom of Jesus ben-Sira, for example, brings its hymn on the glories of Israel's past to a triumphant conclusion in its celebration of the High Priest Onias III, decked out for a temple liturgy, and of his faithful representation of Jewish religion and tradition. The setting is Palestine before the depredations of Antiochus Epiphanes IV, and the perspective is one of confidence that God's purposes for his covenant people have reached their latest expression in the community and worship of the Second Temple.

Other literature, however, looks for a fuller restoration of Israel than has yet taken place. The books of Enoch, Tobit, and the Psalms of Solomon, for example, contain aspirations towards a glorious vindication of Israel from its enemies, in which a major role is played not only by the expected Messiah, but also by the temple. Attitudes to the temple, however, were by no means uniform. Antiochus Epiphanes IV's desecration of it produced, in time, a variety of responses, even among traditional Jews, spanning the militarism of the Hasmonaeans and the

---

11.  I have developed this in 'Jerusalem in the Old Testament', in *Jerusalem Past and Present in the Purposes of God* (ed. P.W.L. Walker; Cambridge: Tyndale House, 1992), pp. 21-51.

withdrawal of the Qumran community. And a well-established Diaspora adds a further dimension to the picture of Judaism in the period between the Old Testament and the first century CE.

The variety in the views of Jerusalem and the temple, in a time which saw much activity in the sphere of biblical interpretation, might be expected to appear in the literature. Since our particular interest is in Deuteronomy's altar-law, we shall review the evidence through that lens. To anticipate the conclusion of this section, we shall find that the orientation of a particular writing strongly affects the way in which the law is read.

This point could hardly be better illustrated by the body of literature that is probably most atypical on the subject, namely the Samaritan Pentateuch. Its tendentious interpretation of the Deuteronomic altar-law in favour of the Samaritan sanctuary at Shechem appears in a number of ways. The interest in Shechem emerges explicitly in Deuteronomy 27, especially in its reading בהר גרזים for בהר עיבל (Deut. 27.4). In the altar-law itself its regular substitution of the perfect form of the verb בחר for the imperfect which features in all other versions is in line with its firm identification of the chosen place as Shechem. This feature, incidentally, may lend some support, albeit negatively, to the contention that the form in which the law is better known is not formulated with a particular location in mind. (SamP's tendency also appears, incidentally, in Leviticus, in its adjustment, in common with other MSS, of the unexpected plural מקדשיכם to the singular מקדשכם, Lev. 26.31).

Before going further, it should be said that any account of Jewish literature between the testaments faces the difficult problem of relative dating of material, and indeed of knowing the precise *Sitz im Leben* of much of it. What follows, therefore, is not an attempt to trace the history of an idea, but only to notice its use in various Jewish writings.

Having entered this caveat, we may turn to the literature which takes it for granted that Jerusalem is the correct place of worship. In such literature citations of the Deuteronomic altar-law naturally assume that it refers to Jerusalem. Tob. 1.4, for example, alludes to the formula, in a book which also appeals to Isaianic prophecies about the city's restoration (Tob. 13–14; cf. Isa. 54, 60). Tobit is probably set in the Diaspora, and expresses a hope for the return of dispersed Jewry to the Holy City. It thus furnishes evidence of the importance of Jerusalem even beyond Palestine.[12]

12.    G.W.E. Nickelsburg, *Jewish Literature between the Bible and the*

The midrashic work on Deuteronomy known as *Sifrê* brings the altar-law into connection with Psalms 132 and 2 Chron 3.1. The relevance of the law to the temple at Jerusalem is assumed, therefore, and indeed the term 'chosen house' in the discussion is further confirmation of this. Yet *Sifrê* contains some interesting reflections on the way in which the law should be read in relation to the history of Israel in the Old Testament. It observes the different expressions 'out of all your tribes' (Deut. 12.5) and 'in one of your tribes' (Deut. 12.14). In the rabbinical discussion that is stimulated by this observation one voice interprets the latter phrase of Shiloh and the former of Jerusalem.[13] The formula in Deut. 12.14 is variously ascribed to the two places.[14] Among other issues debated is the relationship between the Deuteronomic altar-law and that of Exod. 20.21, and the meaning of Deut. 12.8 ('You shall not act as we are acting here today...'). The discussion of the latter passage resorts to the story of Israel's settlement and early life in the land for an explanation, and finds in the passage a justification of high-place worship in the time before the building of the temple.[15]

The interpretations in *Sifrê* hardly amount to systematic exegesis in the modern sense. Nevertheless *Sifrê* highlighted issues in the interpretation of the altar-law which would recur subsequently, and suggested possible directions for it. Most importantly it brought the law into connection with the narrative of the early history of Israel.

The pseudepigraphical *Book of Jubilees* (second century BCE)[16] has features in common with *Sifrê*. Its orientation towards the Jerusalem sanctuary appears at the outset (1.17), as Yahweh reveals to Moses the future history of his people; indeed the building of the temple seems to constitute the meaning and goal of history (1.27-28). *Jubilees* draws eclectically on Deuteronomy and the priestly parts of the Pentateuch; echoes of Deuteronomy's legislation on worship appear, for example, in 32.10-11, both in the idea of a 'second tithe',[17] and in the expression

*Mishnah* (London: SCM Press, 1981), p. 35.

13.   J. Neusner, *Sifrê*, p. 192.

14.   J. Neusner, *Sifrê*, p. 213.

15.   J. Neusner, *Sifrê*, p. 197.

16.   See J.H. Charlesworth (ed.), *The Old Testament Pseudepigrapha* (vol. 2; New York: Doubleday, 1985), pp. 43-44.

17.   On the idea of a second tithe and other interpretations of the relationship between the Pentateuchal tithe-laws, see the present writer's *Law and Theology in Deuteronomy* (JSOTSup, 33; Sheffield: JSOT Press, 1984), pp. 69ff.

'the place where it is determined that his name shall dwell'. *Jub.* 32.23 is also germane.

*Jubilees* has in common with the literature discussed above that it considers the arrangements for worship in the land prior to the building of the temple. It too looks to Deuteronomy and DtH in developing a view:

> And whenever the children of Israel enter the land which they will possess, into the land of Canaan, they will set up the tabernacle of the LORD in the midst of the land, in one of their tribes, until the sanctuary of the LORD is built upon the land. And it will come to pass, when they come and observe the Passover in the midst of the tabernacle of the LORD that they will sacrifice it before the LORD from year to year. And in the days when a house is built in the name of the LORD in the land of their inheritance, they shall go there, and they shall sacrifice the Passover at evening when the sun is setting...[18]

The language is Deuteronomic throughout this passage. But the interpretation of the altar-law is particularly interesting. The phrase 'they shall go there' echoes Deut. 12.5 (even though it is the Passover law that is in view), and is applied to the temple in Jerusalem. In contrast, the phrase 'in one of your tribes' (Deut. 12.14) is applied to the tabernacle wherever it may be set up before the temple is built. Other phrases from Deuteronomy's worship laws are also applied to this period: 'before the LORD'; 'from year to year'; see Deut. 14.22, 15.20 for the latter phrase).

*Jubilees* thus shares a basic approach to Deuteronomy 12 with *Sifrê*, though Shiloh is not named. The 'Shiloh' understanding of the altar-law (that is, the understanding of its application in terms of the story of DtH, even in literature strongly orientated towards Jerusalem) seems to have gained a secure foothold in Jewish literature between the Old Testament and the early Christian centuries. An example from later Jewish interpretation, the commentary of Rashi, confirms its tenacity. Rashi refers the chosen place in Deut. 12.5 to Shiloh, and in vv. 11, 14 to Jerusalem. He also understands the command in Deut. 12.8 ('You shall not act as we are acting here today) as intended to permit sacrifice in a restricted way at high-places *between* the existence of sanctuaries, namely Shiloh, Nob, Gibeon and Jerusalem.[19]

18. Translation of O.S. Wintermute in Charlesworth (ed.), *Pseudepigrapha*.
19. See M. Rosenbaum and A.M. Silbermann, *Pentateuch with Targum Onkelos, Haphtaroth and Prayers for Sabbath, and Rashi's Commentary: Deuteronomy*

The Targum to Deuteronomy, like the literature so far considered, identifies the chosen place explicitly as the Jerusalem temple. Its rendering of Deut. 12.5 (Onkelos) reads: '...but only to the site that the LORD your God will choose amidst all your tribes to establish his *Shekinah*. There you should seek him at the house of his *Shekinah*, there you are to come.'[20] The theology of the *Shekinah* is no doubt accommodated by the Hebrew לשכנו (Deut. 12.5).[21] Onkelos has also in common with *Sifrê* its use of the term 'house' (בית).

The Targum Onkelos (being a fairly straightforward translation) does not overtly raise the question discussed in *Sifrê*, namely whether the altar-law might in any way find an echo in the sanctuary at Shiloh. It is interesting, however, for its theology of the *Shekinah*. The Targum here reflects the attempt of Jewish thinkers to understand the nature of God's presence with his people through the temple cult. This may be seen in places other than Deuteronomy. The Isaiah Targum, furthermore, as B.D. Chilton has shown, contains sophisticated reflection on the relationship between God's presence in the temple and his presence in heaven—a theology which, in time, had to respond to the destruction of the temple.[22] The *Shekinah* is part of a cluster of ideas (including the *memra'*) which focus on God's coming into relationship with human beings.[23]

While the Qumran fragments of Deuteronomy have not revealed anything of special interest to our present purpose, the Temple Scroll deserves notice. Though found at Qumran, the Scroll may emanate from the Jerusalem priesthood of an earlier period.[24] It contains detailed instructions for the building of the temple and the institution of the cult,

(London: Shapiro, Vallantine & Co., 1934), pp. 64ff.; and cf. the Mishnaic tractate *Zeb.* 119a.

20.   The translation here and elsewhere is that of I. Drazin, *Targum Onkelos to Deuteronomy* (New York: Ktav, 1982), p. 144.

21.   L. Laberge, 'Le lieu que YHWH a choisi pour y mettre son Nom: (TM, LXX, Vg, et Targums). Contribution à la critique textuelle d'une formule deutéronomiste', *EstBib* 43 (1985), pp. 213-14.

22.   B.D. Chilton, *The Glory of Israel: The Theology and Provenience of the Isaiah Targum* (JSOTSup, 23; Sheffield: JSOT Press, 1983), pp. 70-71.

23.   B.D. Chilton, *The Glory of Israel*, p. 56.

24.   H. Stegemann, 'The Literary Composition of the Temple Scroll and its Status at Qumran', in *Temple Scroll Studies* (ed. G.J. Brooke; JSPSup, 7; Sheffield: JSOT Press, 1989), p. 131. Cf. M.O. Wise, *A Critical Study of the Temple Scroll from Qumran Cave 11* (Chicago: University of Chicago Press, 1990), p. 200.

together with a law-code. There is disagreement as to whether the Scroll is a programme for 'history' or for 'eschatology'.[25] Most probably, however, it should be read as referring to the temple that was to be built after the conquest of the land. Its language concerning the presence of God has some kinship with that of the later Targums.[26]

One of the Scroll's interesting features is its special use of Deuteronomy 12–26 as the basis of the law-code section.[27] In this context, its handling of the formula concerning the chosen place is striking. The formula appears clearly at certain points (52.8-12, cf. Deut. 15.19-23; 52.13-21, cf. Deut. 12.13-16; 53.9-10, cf. Deut. 12.6; 56.5, cf. Deut. 17.10). It is characterized by the use throughout of the term מקדש instead of Deuteronomy's מקום. This is in line with the Scroll's eclectic use of Pentateuchal texts, and with its assumption that the formula refers to the temple.

It is a curious feature of the Scroll that, although most of the Deuteronomic law-code is represented in it, the majority of the occurrences of the altar-law itself do not appear, because of the Scroll's omission of Deuteronomy 12, 14 and 26.[28] This may be a consequence of the eclectic use of the Pentateuch.[29] It is probably precarious to interpret this 'silence' in the Scroll. However, in the light of our observations on other Jewish literature, it may be that it avoided Deuteronomy 12 because of the difficult questions of interpretation which it raised.

It is important, finally, to consider the Septuagint (LXX). It goes without saying that its translation of the Hebrew Scriptures into Greek for the Jews of Alexandria is an interpretation, which in fact has certain features in common with the Targum, but which also differs from it.

In relation to the altar-law LXX exhibits a strong tendency, over against MT, to harmonize the formula. For example, the difference

25. See the references in J. Maier, *The Temple Scroll* (JSOTSup, 34; Sheffield: JSOT Press, 1985), p. 86.

26. 11QTemple 29.8-9 uses שכן (hi.) with the term 'Glory', as do Neofiti and Ps.-Jon. on Deuteronomy12.5; see Laberge, 'Le lieu', p. 213.

27. The relationship between the Scroll's law-code and existing law-codes is not clear. Some think of it as a kind of replacement for others, and the whole Scroll as a new Torah; see Stegemann, 'Literary Composition', pp. 138-39.

28. Stegemann thinks the omission of ch. 26 may be accidental ('Literary Composition', pp. 138-39). See in contrast, however, Wise, *Temple Scroll*, p. 200.

29. Stegemann's suggestion that Deuteronomy12 has effectively been replaced by cols. 3-47 of the Scroll, which draw on the 'priestly' parts of the Pentateuch, is attractive.

between the phrase 'out of all your tribes' (12.5) and 'in one of your tribes' (12.14), which attracts attention in rabbinical discussion, is ignored in LXX, which renders both expressions ἐν μιᾷ τῶν φυλακῶν. (This has the effect, incidentally, of removing the ambiguity of MT about whether a single sanctuary is meant, or one per tribe.[30])

The most important feature of its rendering of the formula, however, is that it regularly uses the term ἐπικαλοῦμαι to render both שכן and שום in connection with the name of Yahweh at the sanctuary. This expression is clearly not a direct translation of either Hebrew verb, and is, as might be expected, more commonly used to render the Hebrew קרא (ni.). The significance of LXX's choice has been interpreted in a number of ways. L. Laberge sees it as part of a tendency in post-biblical Judaism to express the presence of God at the sanctuary. He postulates a progression within LXX, in respect of the altar-law formula, which finishes with the translation of שכן by κατασκηνόω in Jer. 7.12. The use of the passive of ὁράω in Exod. 25.8, for Hebrew שכן, is seen in the same context.[31] In his view, therefore, LXX exhibits theological characteristics similar to those in the Targums.

It is preferable, however, to see in LXX a rather different kind of concern from that of the Targums. Laberge underestimates the importance of LXX's avoidance of direct translations of שכן in Deuteronomy (and the Pentateuch in general). And his assumption that the ideas underlying the 'calling of Yahweh's name', and his being 'seen' at the sanctuary, are similar to the Targums' Shekinah is not sufficiently examined. Rather, with C. Dogniez and M. Harl, it is better to suppose that LXX wants to suggest that the name is merely pronounced over the sanctuary, possibly guarding against the idea of Yahweh's actual presence, in an exclusive, or even 'sacral', way.[32] There is indeed other evidence of a universalizing and spiritualizing interest in Deuteronomy LXX, consistent presumably with its setting outside the land of Israel (though in contrast with Tobit).[33] Furthermore, in a somewhat analogous feature to its

30.  See further below.

31.  L. Laberge, 'Le lieu', pp. 226-34.

32.  C. Dogniez and M. Harl, *Le Deutéronome* (La Bible d'Alexandrie, 5; Paris: Les Editions d'Cerf, 1992), p. 194. They appeal to 1 Kgs 8.26-30, which they understand to remove the presence of God from the sanctuary itself.

33.  For example, it reads ἐπὶ τῆς γῆς for MT's land-specific אדמתך at 12.19. In addition, the גר becomes a προσήλυτος (14.29), apparently a coinage of LXX, attesting to proselytism as a phenomenon in third century BCE Alexandrian Judaism (see C. van Houten, *The Alien in Israelite Law* [JSOTSup, 107; Sheffield, JSOT

treatment of the altar-law, Deuteronomy LXX makes the priest serve, not Yahweh directly, but *in the name of* Yahweh (17.12).[34]

*Findings from Old Testament and Jewish Interpretation*
In the literature after Deuteronomy (apart from SamP) the identification of the place as Jerusalem is not at issue. In both Old Testament literature and later Jewish writings, however, the belief is also found that the formula had an application to Shiloh before Jerusalem. In the Old Testament, that application carried with it a note of warning. The status of Jerusalem as the chosen place could not be taken as a permanent given; Yahweh, in his disposal over history and his people's life, retained his freedom.

Later Jewish adaptation of the 'Shiloh' view does not have quite the same form, arising rather from exegetical concern about the legitimacy of worship before the temple was built. Nevertheless, Jewish thinking about divine presence had also to reckon with judgment, supremely with the fall of the temple in 70 CE. And the literature which we have considered, in its assimilation of the idea of a chosen place, shows a concern for the nature of the divine presence there. The Targums, as we have seen, have a developed view of the relationship between the dwelling of God on earth and in heaven. Classically, the Shekinah was an attempt to understand how God may be at once in heaven and among his people on earth. However, the idea allowed for shifts of emphasis. In some passages, the true locus of the Shekinah seems to be heaven (as in the Targum on Isa. 6.3, 6). This emphasis may have been precipitated by the events of 70 CE. After that time, furthermore, the rabbis could even locate the Shekinah at their academic centres.[35]

LXX, in a quite different way, has reflected on the nature of the divine presence at the temple, and in its adaptation of the idea of the 'name' of Yahweh there, has apparently wanted to avoid a crude concept of it.

---

Press, 1991], pp. 179-83). Finally, the prohibition of work on the last day of the Passover expressly permits those works ὅσα ποιηθήσεται ψυχῇ (16.8).

34. In this place MT has לשרת שם את יהוה and LXX reads: λειτουργεῖν ἐπὶ τῷ ὀνόματι τοῦ κυρίου τοῦ θεοῦ σου.

35. Chilton, *Glory of Israel*, pp. 70-73; cf. M. Goldberg, *Untersuchungen über die Vorstellung von der Schekhinah in der frühen rabbinischen Literatur* (StJ, 5; Berlin: de Gruyter, 1969).

*The New Testament*

The New Testament has much to say about the temple because of its special claims about the person of Jesus. A full review of its understanding of 'place', and of the Jerusalem temple in particular, is impossible in the present context. Because the topic is of fundamental importance in the New Testament, the study of it cannot be reduced to its interpretation of a single text. In fact there is no clear allusion to the Deuteronomic altar-law. However, one passage comes very close to this, namely the speech of Stephen, on the verge of his martyrdom, as it is recorded in Acts 7. Because it does, and because of the tenor of his argument, it is in place to consider it briefly as one further angle on the understanding of the temple in the first Christian century.

The speech has in common with some Old Testament passages (such as Ps. 78, discussed above) its critical review of Israel's history. It focuses especially on Moses, no doubt because of the accusation that Stephen had uttered 'blasphemous words' against Moses and God (Acts 6.11). Yet Stephen begins the story with Abraham (7.2) and traces it through to Solomon and the building of the temple (7.47). The sweep through history corresponds in Stephen's presentation to the movement of God, who brought his people out of Egypt, and into the land, carrying with them the 'tent of testimony' (ἡ σκηνὴ τοῦ μαρτυρίου) which God had ordered Moses to make in the wilderness (vv. 44-45). Stephen alludes to David's request to build a dwelling-place for God (v. 46). The phrase used there, namely εὑρεῖν σκήνωμα τῷ οἴκῳ Ἰακώβ, is quoted loosely from Ps. 132.5 (LXX), which in turn reflects the Deuteronomic idea of 'seeking' a place for worship of Yahweh. (Stephen, interestingly, says τῷ οἴκῳ instead of LXX τῷ θεῷ, focusing more directly on the temple than the phrase in the Psalm.[36] His choice of term presumably reflects the influence of 2 Sam. 7.8-16, which is the main source for this part of his story). It is clear, however, that the tent is definitive for Stephen, rather than the temple, for the building of the latter is adduced only to recall the prophetic critique of false confidence placed in it as a building in Isa. 66.1-2 (vv. 49-50). The 'house/building' motif, which Stephen develops in vv. 47-48, leads suitably into the citation of this text.

Stephen's idea of a temple 'not made with human hands' is not unique to him in early Christian critique of Jewish worship. It occurs also

36.   Cf., however, v. 3 of the Psalm, LXX, where the phrase σκήνωμα οἴκου μου appears.

in the letter to the Hebrews. The thought of that epistle about the temple is not exactly like Stephen's, as it uses the tabernacle rather more as a 'shadow' of Christ.[37] Yet there are similarities. Indeed, according to W. Manson, writing about the tabernacle in Hebrews, 'the tent was a type or figure of God's never-ceasing, never-halted appointments for his people's salvation'.[38] The appraisal might also apply to Stephen's view in the sense that he has pictured a history of God with his people that is always moving forward, and which did not reach a conclusion in the building of the temple. This view, as we have seen, was neither new nor exclusively Christian. Rather, it was already available to Stephen in Old Testament thought, as it was to contemporary Jewish writers.

*Modern Interpretations*

In modern study, the altar-law lies at the heart of interpretations of Deuteronomy as a whole. As we shall see, the identification of the 'place' as Jerusalem is not the end, but only the beginning, of the interpretation of the book, and brings profound theological implications in its train. There are, as we shall see, interesting analogies between ancient and modern interpretations. We must begin, however, by setting modern study of the law in its historical context.

Modern thinking about of the altar-law, like ancient treatments, began with an assumption about the identity of the chosen place. De Wette put the relationship between the altar-law and other Pentateuchal legislation back on the agenda in 1805, noting both the prominence of the law in Deuteronomy and the contrast which it made with legislation in the first four Pentateuchal books, typified by Exod. 20.24-25. Deuteronomy's concept, he believed, replaced the earlier one, and was put into effect by Josiah. De Wette's identification of the Book of the Law (2 Kgs 22.8) as Deuteronomy was an important and influential part of his thesis.[39] For Wellhausen, the altar-law of Deuteronomy must be dated in the time of Josiah's reform, in connection with the polemic of the Books of Kings

---

37. But see F.F. Bruce, *The Book of the Acts* (Grand Rapids: Eerdmans, 1954), p. 143, n. 20.

38. W. Manson, *The Epistle to the Hebrews* (London: Hodder & Stoughton, 1951), pp. 33-34.

39. He regarded the law of Lev. 17, requiring slaughter at the tabernacle only, also as late and 'non-Mosaic'; W.M.L. de Wette, *Dissertatio Critica* (Jena, 1805), pp. 13-14; and see M.J. Paul, *Het Archimedisch Punt van de Pentateuchkritik* ('s-Gravenhage: Boekencentrum, 1988), pp. 76-79. Note, incidentally, Paul's belief that de Wette had antecedents in modern times, including Voltaire (pp. 79-80).

against local sanctuaries and in favour, as he saw it, of Jerusalem.[40] The Old Testament's occasional application of the place-formula to Shiloh was, in Wellhausen's view, the invention of a later generation which saw the sanctuary there as a forerunner of the Jerusalem temple.[41]

Wellhausen's theory, however, raised a theological, or religious, question. What precise theological motivation lay behind the concentration of worship in Jerusalem, according to his view? In part, it consisted of a polemic against worship at the so-called high-places. That being so, it was to some extent a victory of the Jerusalem priesthood over rival claimants, who appear in the Deuteronomic literature as 'priests of the high-places'. Was it, therefore, a blow for a certain kind of cultic religion? Wellhausen himself apparently thought so.

Wellhausen's treatment of the relationship between D and P was dominated by historical questions. For him the relationship between the two documents consisted primarily in their attitudes to centralization: while D demanded it, P simply presupposed it.[42] This concern assumes a certain continuity between them. Wellhausen saw, however, that a theological question arose too, and thought that Deuteronomy began to challenge a 'sacral' understanding of religion and sacrifice which had characterized earlier religion in Israel.[43] Subsequent studies also postulated a distinction between the relatively more 'sacral' theology attributed to older sources and to P, and Deuteronomy's view, which was said to be less bound by those concepts. Noth, for example, could see Leviticus 17 as an attempt to reverse D's permission to slaughter non-sacrificially, and thus as a return to a concept of sacral slaughter which he found in 1 Sam. 14.30-35.

The paradox here will be readily apparent. On the one hand Deuteronomy promotes the interests of a sanctuary; on the other it is said to be a deliberate move away from 'sacral' religion. The problem which faces the interpreter here has several aspects. Not least of these are the exegetical questions which emerge from the altar-law itself in its

---

40. J. Wellhausen, *Prolegomena to the History of Israel* (Edinburgh: A. & C. Black, 1885), pp. 32-34.

41. Wellhausen, *Prolegomena*, p. 19. As we have seen, later Jewish writing did indeed take over the Shiloh interpretation from the Old Testament. However, as we also saw, its concerns were not the same as those of the Old Testament, notably Jeremiah's insistence on the freedom of Yahweh.

42. Wellhausen, *Prolegomena*, p. 35.

43. See my *Law and Theology*, p. 43.

various occurrences and immediate contexts. However, it is important to notice first that the interpretation of Deuteronomy's attitude to the altar-law and cultic things in particular is only part of the wider understanding of the book as a whole. The ambiguity over the book's attitude to the cult is in the context of an ambiguity about its attitude to politics and the monarchy.

At the centre of this question is Deuteronomy's attitude to kingship. The book speaks explicitly about this only at 17.14-20, in a law which permits, but does not require, the people to appoint a king, on condition that he remain subject to the law, and remember that he is a 'brother'-Israelite. This law has been read variously as an affirmation of kingship and as critical of it. In favour of the former view is the association of Deuteronomy with Josiah's reform. Some have argued that any reform of religion in favour of Jerusalem must promote in some way the existing Jerusalem traditions. These include a strong association of king and cult, as celebrated most notably in the Zion Psalms.[44] M. Weinfeld also thought Deuteronomy stood close to the royal court, though on different grounds, namely its affinities with wisdom literature.[45]

On the other hand, Deuteronomy has affinities with strands of Old Testament literature which are not obviously hospitable to royal and sacral ideas. The nexus which stretches from Samuel and Elijah through Hosea to Jeremiah has been characterized as northern and covenantal ('Ephraimite', to use R.R. Wilson's term).[46] Its prophetic spirit and covenantal rationale contrasts with the pro-monarchical stance of Jerusalem. Deuteronomy's hostility to Canaanite religion, together with its covenantal spirit, seems to place it close to such literature.

The attempt, then, to place Deuteronomy in relation to the traditions of Israel can lead in quite different directions. It is easy to see, further-more, how features of the book could be drafted on both sides of this argument. It apparently centralizes worship, and is connected in DtH with Josiah's reform; yet it conspicuously omits to name Jerusalem. It permits the appointment of a king, though a rationale evidently existed

---

44. R.E. Clements, 'Deuteronomy and the Jerusalem Cult Tradition', *VT* 15 (1965), pp. 300-12.

45. M. Weinfeld, *Deuteronomy and the Deuteronomic School* (Oxford: Clarendon, 1972), pp. 166-71.

46. R.R. Wilson, *Prophecy in Ancient Israel* (Philadelphia: Fortess Press, 1980). See also E.W. Nicholson, *Deuteronomy and Tradition* (Oxford: Blackwell, 1967), pp. 58-82.

in Israel for opposition to this (Deut. 33.5; Judg. 8.22-23; 1 Sam. 8.7); yet the conditions laid down for a king are so constrictive as to make the institution virtually unrecognizable in terms of ancient Near Eastern expectations. It will readily be seen, furthermore, that this apparent ambivalence in the book is congruent with that which has been noticed above concerning its view of the cult. The tendency to align Deuteronomy with the Jerusalem traditions puts it on the side of a sacral theology; a covenantal interpretation, on the other hand, stresses rather the spiritual and ethical in its religion.

The problem, thus perceived, has been addressed in a number of ways. Von Rad resolved it by supposing that the altar-law was no original part of Deuteronomy, and foreign to its essential spirit.[47] Others, granting that the altar-law does properly belong to the book, invoke some form of assimilation of the two kinds of concepts. R.E. Clements thinks of a 'demythologization' of the ancient Jerusalem traditions by the authors of Deuteronomy, as an explanation of the acceptance of 'northern' traditions by the Jerusalem authorities. On this view the attitude to Jerusalem is altered from the old mythico-cultic view to one which—while allowing the claims of Jerusalem to primacy—affirmed that Yahweh dwelt not on earth (i.e. in the temple) but in heaven.[48] The idea of demythologization was developed at length by M. Weinfeld, who saw centralization as a crucial part of a de-sacralizing programme applied to the Jerusalem traditions.[49] E.W. Nicholson, while questioning whether Deuteronomy was as polemically orientated towards the Jerusalem traditions, agreed that there were elements of compromise between northern and southern religious conceptions.[50] The element of compromise thus identified in the promulgation of Deuteronomy is believed to explain the reticence of the book about naming Jerusalem, though the scholars concerned have no doubt that that city is indeed intended by the altar-law.

The above treatments have tried to interpret the altar-law in terms which in some sense assimilated Deuteronomy's central concerns to the interests of Jerusalem. B. Halpern has recently attempted something similar, in a new way. In Halpern's view, the chief aim of centralization was to effect a social revolution, challenging the ancient patriarchal

---

47. G. von Rad, *Studies in Deuteronomy* (London: SCM Press, 1953), p. 67.
48. R.E. Clements, 'Jerusalem Cult Tradition'.
49. M. Weinfeld, *Deuteronomic School*, pp. 9, 51-58, 158-61.
50. E.W. Nicholson, *Deuteronomy*, pp. 103-106.

structure of Israel, with its tribes, clans and 'fathers' houses'.[51] This happened under pressure from Assyria, both in terms of contemporary currents of thought in the wider world, but also as a strategy for defence.[52] In the process, Judah was transformed from a traditional society to an elitist, individualistic one.[53]

Halpern thus proposes, or presupposes, a marriage between centralization as a political measure and the Deuteronomic/prophetic movement as a theological programme. In his view Deuteronomy and the Books of Kings portray what was merely traditional Israelite religion as idolatrous and treacherous (Deut. 13).[54] At the same time, the prophets, together with Josiah, are seen as the true creators both of moral individualism (reflected in Deuteronomy's use of the second person singular address[55]), and 'aniconic monotheism':

> And Josiah's Puritan aniconism, and Jeremiah's radical monotheism both presuppose the same ideology, the very ideology that produced the doctrine of moral individuation; monism, the one and not the many, was the order of the day. [56]

Halpern's thesis has in common with the other studies which we have just noted the attempt to reconcile 'spiritualizing' tendencies in Deuteronomy with its demand for centralization. Its specific historical reconstruction is new, as are its sociological categories. In this sense it is supported by P. Dion's analysis of Deuteuteronomy 13, in which he claims that the concern of that chapter is to promote the new view against any recrudescence of the old ways.[57] Deuteronomy is thus characterized as 'statist'. In this way, the idea of centralization is refined, and made an instrument of a penetrating sociological revolution, which ultimately laid the foundations for modern ideas about the individual's

---

51. B. Halpern, 'Jerusalem and the Lineages in the Seventh Century BCE: Kinship and the Rise of Individual Moral Liability', in *Law and Ideology in Ancient Israel* (ed. B. Halpern and D.W. Hobson; JSOTSup, 124; Sheffield: JSOT Press, 1991), pp. 11-107; see his description of the traditional social organization; pp. 50ff.

52. Halpern, 'Jerusalem and the Lineages', pp. 21-27, cf. 41ff.

53. Halpern, 'Jerusalem and the Lineages', pp. 59ff.

54. Halpern, 'Jerusalem and the Lineages', pp. 74-75; cf. P.E. Dion, 'Deuteronomy 13: The Suppression of Alien Religious Propaganda during the Late Monarchical Era', in *Law and Ideology* (ed. Halpern), pp. 147-216.

55. Halpern, 'Jerusalem and the Lineages', p. 75.

56. Halpern, 'Jerusalem and the Lineages', p. 81.

57. Dion, 'Deuteronomy 13'.

ethical responsibility and relationship to society. It is an interesting
attempt to resolve the ambivalence which Deuteronomy study has tried
to cope with since Wellhausen, namely between the assertion of central
control and the bid for personal and religious freedom, because it avoids
the need for concepts like accommodation and compromise espoused by
Clements and Nicholson. It is nevertheless in line with their treatments,
in the sense that the interpretation of the book has been dominated by
the belief that it serves the interests of state and sanctuary. The question
whether it succeeds must await the result of exegetical considerations
which follow.

## 2. *Interpretation of the Altar-Law: Exegetical Issues*

The problem of interpretation lies in the first instance in the language of
Deuteronomy itself, and particularly in the terms used in connection
with the altar-law. The question how Deuteronomy relates to Josiah's
reform begins, naturally, with the fact that Jerusalem is not named by
the formula. Could it actually refer to another location, such as Shechem,
named in the ceremony prescribed in Deuteronomy 27? Interest is
added to the detective-game by the phrase 'out of all your tribes' (v. 5),
with its intriguing variation ('in one of your tribes' v. 14). Could the
formula refer to more than one place? Or is there some special reason
for the omission of the name? If so, is it merely superficial—the need to
avoid anachronism—and the reference to Jerusalem taken for granted?
Or in contrast, is there a deeper purpose in the mind of the lawgiver for
his refusal to identify the law closely with a particular place?

  Other exegetical questions follow. When it is said that Yahweh will
'put his name' at the place, should this be understood within the framework of a relatively 'sacral' theology, or as a device of a desacralizing
programme? Similarly, does the expression 'before the LORD'
(Deut. 12.7) imply a real encounter with God in the cult-place, or is it
merely a relic of the more sacral view? And are other features of the
language (the verb שכן, for example), at home in the Jerusalem cult
tradition? ('Sacral' ideas, in this discussion, are those which are said to
portray the deity in anthropomorphic, corporeal terms, as if he were
present at the place of worship in a virtually tangible way. Conversely,
'desacralizing' ideas conceive of God in much more abstract terms).[58]

---

58.  For a fuller definition along these lines, see Weinfeld, *Deuteronomic School*,
pp. 191-93.

It hardly needs saying that these questions have been answered very differently in the interests of different global views of Deuteronomy. We have already noticed the contrary tendencies within the interpretation of Deuteronomy made popular by Wellhausen. It is clear that in any attempt to resolve the tensions involved in trying to relate the book to the reform, decisions have to be made on the exegetical questions just raised. It is time to consider such attempts.

## The Name of Yahweh

In the theory that Deuteronomy saw an accommodation between conflicting traditions, an interpretation of its 'name theology' played a part. According to that interpretation, articulated by von Rad and promoted by Schreiner and Weinfeld among others, the idea of Yahweh's setting his name at the place of worship was a device to guard his transcendence, that is, the belief that his dwelling was in heaven, not in the sanctuary.

Von Rad thought that Deuteronomy's concept of the divine dwelling at the sanctuary showed a development compared with the older idea found at Exod. 20.24. There too the name of Yahweh was associated with his presence. But in Deuteronomy it has become 'a constant, almost material presence of the name at the shrine', such as 'verges closely upon a hypostasis'.[59] This theology has a polemical element, intending to replace 'the old crude idea of Jahweh's presence and dwelling at the shrine by a theologically sublimated idea'.[60]

The idea of a Deuteronomic repudiation of older concepts is developed at greater length by Weinfeld. For him too, pre-Deuteronomic texts think of Yahweh in an anthropomorphic way, as actually present in the sanctuary, and in this respect P has preserved the more ancient view.[61] Like von Rad he thinks that Deuteronomy has consciously altered the meaning of older usage. The phrase 'put the name' itself has antecedents in the El Amarna letters (Akk. *sakan sumsu*, cf. Heb. שׂכֵן שׁם), where it occurs in royal inscriptions and apparently implies a claim to ownership. Weinfeld argues, however, against de Vaux, that that original meaning is superseded in Deuteronomy which uses it to convey an abstract notion of God.[62]

---

59. G. von Rad, *Studies in Deuteronomy* (London: SCM Press, 1953), p. 38.
60. Von Rad, *Studies in Deuteronomy*, p. 39.
61. Weinfeld, *Deuteronomic School*, p. 192.
62. Weinfeld, *Deuteronomic School*, pp. 193-94; cf. R. de Vaux, 'Le lieu que

He goes on to support his view by exegetical considerations. The Deuteronomic school uses the vocabulary of the name of Yahweh consistently, he claims. There is no case of God himself being said to dwell in the temple; rather the temple is always the dwelling of his name. The most important text for Weinfeld is 1 Kings 8, where in Solomon's prayer of dedication of the temple, the phrase 'your dwelling place' (מקום שבתך) is always accompanied by the phrase 'in heaven'. Weinfeld contrasts this usage with earlier sources, where God's dwelling place is the sanctuary (Exod. 15.17). This very phrase occurs within Solomon's prayer, in the ascription of praise which opens it (vv. 12-13). Weinfeld thinks it is clear, however, that the Deuteronomist rejects that concept by means of all that follows. He finds a similar conflict between Dtr and his source in 2 Sam. 7.5-7, 13a.[63] Furthermore, Deuteronomy itself embodies the concept found in 1 Kings 8 at Deut. 26.19.[64]

The interpretations of von Rad and Weinfeld, however, are questionable on exegetical grounds. The language about Yahweh's name in Deuteronomy 12 and similar texts is in the first instance a claim for his legitimacy in contrast to that of other gods (vv. 3-5). In this respect de Vaux's insistence on the relevance of the El Amarna data is correct. Furthermore, the name of Yahweh is elsewhere closely connected with his identity and being, notably in Exod. 3.13-14 and in certain Psalms.[65] There is, indeed, a language of devotion in the Psalms in which the 'name' finds a natural place, which suggests that the 'name' phraseology is not precisely about the nature of presence, but rather about the nature of God.[66] The polemic in Deuteronomy is certainly against the whole religious system of Canaan, but it is specifically about the exclusive claims of Yahweh himself.

Yahvé a choisi pour y établir son nom', in *Das Ferne und Nahe Wort* (FS L. Rost; BZAW, 105; Berlin: de Gruyter, 1967), pp. 219-28.

63. Weinfeld, *Deuteronomic School*, pp. 193-96.

64. Weinfeld, *Deuteronomic School*, p. 198.

65. E.g. Ps. 68.5a (EVV 4a).

66. See J.G. McConville, 'God's Name and God's Glory', *TynBul* 30 (1979), pp. 156-57. Von Rad argued that the terms 'name' and 'glory' represented different ways of denying God's immediate presence at the sanctuary, the latter removing it more thoroughly (*Studies*, p. 39). In the article cited, I argue that the two terms have rather different functions from each other. 'Glory' occurs more frequently in contexts which have to do with the manifestation of God's presence. The Psalms, incidentally, if Ps. 11.4 is representative, easily accept the dwelling of Yahweh both in heaven and at the sanctuary.

Weinfeld's theory depends on other readings which may be challenged. It is not clear that the prayer of Solomon intends to challenge the concept found in its opening lines. This belief seems to be forced by the theory. In fact it too depends on the misconception that what is at stake in the adoption of name theology is 'crude' or 'anthropomorphic' notions of God's presence. The passages in question, in my view, have more to do with the attempt to conceive of the paradox of Yahweh's transcendence, or his dwelling in heaven, while he can also be said to be among his people on earth. This being so, they stand along with others such as Exod. 33.18-23,[67] and the striking near-juxtaposition of Exod. 19.20 and 20.22.[68] The significance of the invocation to God in heaven in Deut. 26.19 is also to be understood in this context, as I shall argue further below.

It is by no means obvious, therefore, that the Deuteronomic name theology signifies a deliberate assertion of divine transcendence over against conceptions which located him crudely in the sanctuary. This sort of polarization does too little justice to the thinking of the Old Testament writers, even those supposed to be relatively 'old'. A very similar point will emerge from a consideration of the phrase 'before the LORD', also typical of the altar-law, which follows next.

## Presence of God

Our attempt to understand the meaning of Deuteronomy's altar-law has thus taken us necessarily into exegetical and theological questions about its concept of God's presence. The need for precision in this area is clear from the conflicting interpretations of 'name theology' which we have already observed.

It is widely held that Deuteronomy differs significantly from other Pentateuchal sources in relation to divine presence. In its alleged emphasis on the transcendence of Yahweh, Deuteronomy is said to differ most seriously from P, with its corporeal idea of God and

---

67. J. Barr has argued that this passage has nothing to do with anthropomorphic conceptions of God, but rather about the relationship between sin and the transcendence of God: 'Theophany and Anthropomorphism in the Old Testament', in *Congress Volume, Oxford 1959* (ed. J.A. Emerton *et al.*; VTSup, 7; Leiden: Brill, 1959), pp. 31-38 (36). In this passage, incidentally, the terms 'name' and 'glory' both occur. See McConville, 'God's Name and God's Glory', pp. 154-55.

68. See Weinfeld, *Deuteronomic School*, pp. 206-207 n. 4; and further below.

consequent belief in his actual presence in the tabernacle or temple.[69] Besides 'name theology', two principal features of Deuteronomy are invoked to support the view that Deuteronomy is rejecting this. First, Deuteronomy omits the account in Exod. 19.11, 20 of Yahweh's descent on Mt Sinai. The significance of this is explained by means of an interpretation of Deut. 4.36, which is said to distinguish between Yahweh's actual dwelling in heaven, and the hearing of his words on earth.[70] Secondly, it records his speech to the people from the mountain, playing down the visual element. In Weinfeld's words, Deuteronomy 'has taken care to shift the centre of gravity of the theophany from the visual to the aural plane'. Deut. 4.32 is cited as a significant adaptation of an existing tradition in this direction.[71]

A potential problem for this understanding of Deuteronomy is its frequent use of the expression לפני יהוה with its apparent implication of the actual presence of God and a spatial relationship between him and the worshipper. This is met by Mettinger with the observation that it may be a 'linguistic fossil, bearing no semantic cargo of importance'.[72] Others felt a need to distinguish between the ideas of divine presence in Deuteronomy's theologies of Holy War and of the cult, the former presupposing an actual presence with the people (Deut. 7.12).[73]

This synthesis has received severe criticism in the recent work of I. Wilson. By dint of careful comparison of parallel passages in Deuteronomy and other Pentateuchal sources, Wilson shows that Deuteronomy, far from deliberately avoiding terminology that suggests divine presence, in many places actually betrays a heightened interest in it. This he does first for the 'framework', especially chs. 1–3, 4–5, 9–10.[74] In doing so, he questions the exegesis of passages which aim to

---

69. Weinfeld, *Deuteronomic School*, pp. 206-208; cf. T.N.D. Mettinger, *The Dethronement of Sabaoth* (ConBOT, 18; Lund: Gleerup, 1982), p. 124.

70. Weinfeld, *Deuteronomic School*, pp. 206-207; Mettinger, *The Dethronement of Sabaoth*, p. 48.

71. Weinfeld, *Deuteronomic School*, pp. 207-208.

72. Mettinger, *Dethronement of Sabaoth*, p. 53.

73. See Nicholson, *Deuteronomy*, p. 73 n.1; von Rad, *Studies*, pp. 45-59.

74. I. Wilson, 'Divine Presence in Deuteronomy' (PhD thesis, Cambridge University, 1992, forthcoming in SBLDS). For example, Deuteronomy's account of the journey from Sinai to the promised land (1.19-40) contains more indications of Yahweh's actual presence with the people than the parallel Num. 13.1–14.38; he notes especially the references to Yahweh's 'localizations' on the way: 1.33, cf. 1.30 (pp. 29-30).

demonstrate a Deuteronomic theology of transcendence, showing for example, that Deut. 4.36 (a key passage for the 'transcendence' view) actually locates Yahweh both in heaven and on earth.[75] (We shall return to this passage below.) He also rightly questions the logic which says that because the visual aspect of the encounter with Yahweh is muted the 'absence' of Yahweh is implied.[76] In any case, the theory of Yahweh's transcendence underestimates the force of the repeated assertion that the people saw a great fire and heard Yahweh's voice from the midst of it.[77]

Wilson's most important contribution concerns the expression לפני יהוה. While this expression is usually taken to imply the actual presence of Yahweh in P,[78] it cannot be so taken in Deuteronomy by advocates of Deuteronomic transcendence. However, the frequent connection between the expression and the altar-law,[79] together with analogy and a plain reading of the text (with its implication of actual events in time and space),[80] make it unlikely that the author of the laws about the cult was concerned to oppose the idea of Yahweh's real presence. Deut. 26.15, moreover, which speaks of Yahweh's dwelling in heaven, should be understood in the light of Deut. 4.36, where his dwelling there does not rule out his presence on earth also.[81] Wilson believes, in the light of these considerations, that the expression goes further than merely to indicate the chosen place as a location, but implies the personal presence of the deity.[82]

To the observations of Wilson may be added those of P.P. Jenson. Jenson is primarily concerned with the divine presence (among other cultic topics) in the theology of the priestly writings. He argues that, in the cultic thought and practice that lie behind the biblical texts, there are gradations of holiness. This means that the relationship between terms used and the underlying ideas must be carefully explored. On the idea of the presence of God, he takes issue with von Rad, who, in making a distinction between *Präsenztheologie* and *Erscheinungstheologie*, found

---

75. Wilson, 'Divine Presence', pp. 71-72.

76. Wilson, 'Divine Presence', pp. 69, 104-110.

77. Wilson, 'Divine Presence', pp. 80-83.

78. M.D. Fowler, 'The Meaning of lipnê YHWH in the Old Testament', *ZAW* 99 (1987), pp. 384-90 (esp. 387); see further Wilson, 'Divine Presence', p. 152. n. 3.

79. Cf. McConville, 'God's Name and God's Glory', p. 159, n. 41.

80. Wilson, 'Divine Presence', pp. 183-84.

81. Wilson, 'Divine Presence', p. 183.

82. Wilson, 'Divine Presence', pp. 180-81.

the latter to predominate in the priestly writings.[83] In Jenson's view, these should be seen, not as alternative possibilities, but as different aspects of divine presence, that is, static and dynamic. Reviewing the priestly terms for presence, he thinks that some suggest static presence (לפני יהוה, לחם הפנים, משכן), and tend to assure Israelites of their permanent access to Yahweh, while others, like the appearance of Yahweh over the cover of the ark on the Day of Atonement, are dynamic. Such occurrences stress that Yahweh can still meet his people in special ways. The priestly theology of presence, therefore, cannot easily be reduced to a single perspective, but admits of a paradox.[84]

Jenson's observations have implications for our study of Deuteronomy. First, like Wilson, he has supposed that the expression לפני יהוה belongs among the vocabulary that speaks of Yahweh's presence at the sanctuary. Secondly, he has highlighted the possibility of paradox in conceptions of divine presence. The priestly writing has its way of handling the elusive problem of how Yahweh may be thought of as present yet as 'coming'. This, it seems, is a topic inherent for Israel in the attempt to articulate its relationship with God. In respect of P's relationship with Deuteronomy, two things follow, I believe. On the one hand, there is no reason to oppose P and Deuteronomy on the grounds of distinct views of God's presence in the cult, since P itself knows that it is handling a theological paradox. On the other, there is no reason to suppose, *a priori*, that Deuteronomy's language about presence must promote a systematic, polemical view. It is only by such a supposition, I think, that the expression לפני יהוה can be evacuated of what, on a natural reading, it appears to have conveyed in Israel's thinking about presence. It is perfectly possible that Deuteronomy too admits of a paradox similar to that in P on a topic which is by its nature complex. If Wilson has shown that one cannot distinguish between Deuteronomy and P on the grounds of terms used for presence, Jenson directs our attention to the inherent likelihood of paradox in attempts to understand the topic. This observation, finally, is in line with our observations about post-biblical interpretations of the Deuteronomic altar-law.

    83.  Von Rad, 'Zelt und Lade', *NKZ* 42 (1931), pp. 476-98 (= 'The Tent and the Ark', in *The Problem of the Hexateuch and other Essays* [London: SCM Press, 1966]), pp. 103-24.
    84.  P.P. Jenson, *Graded Holiness* (JSOTSup, 106; Sheffield: JSOT Press, 1992), pp. 112-14.

## The Chosen Place

In interpretation of the altar-law that part of it which refers to the 'place which the LORD your God will choose' has excited the most debate. We have seen already how classical criticism has associated the 'place' with Jerusalem, and this association has been one of the decisive factors in what has come to be the dominant critical view of the book. The interpretation of the 'place formula' itself clearly lies also at the centre of our own present interest, namely an understanding of time and place in Deuteronomy. It is time, therefore, to re-evaluate the formula, in the light of our observations so far about other parts of the altar-law.

The formula occurs in slightly different forms, namely:

'the place which the LORD your God will choose out of all your
tribes(מכל שבטיכם)', 12.5;
'the place which the LORD (your God)/he will choose', 12.11, 18, 26, etc.;
'the place which the LORD your God will choose in one of your
tribes(באחד שבטיך)', 12.14. [85]

Regarding the interpretation of the formula, a number of possibilities exist. First, with Wellhausen and others, the place may simply be identified as Jerusalem, and the formula may be understood in connection with Josiah's reform. Secondly, it may refer to some other place, or indeed a succession of places. Furthermore, the identification of the place leaves other questions open, especially whether the formula insists on one sole legitimate sanctuary. That in turn suggests a further possibility, namely, that the different forms of the formula may answer the above questions differently. Does 12.14, for example, permit a number of sanctuaries, while 12.5 insists on only one?

I have reviewed some of these options elsewhere.[86] Several northern sanctuaries have been proposed as the original referent of the formula.[87]

---

85. A further distinction may also be made on the basis of the verb used, i.e. שכן (12.5) or שום (12.21). See B. Halpern, 'The Centralization Formula in Deuteronomy', *VT* 31 (1981), pp. 20-38, who thinks that the latter usage is later. His arguments depend on literary-critical reconstructions of Deut. 12 which I have elsewhere criticized (*Law and Theology*, pp. 40-67). I see no important distinction between the two verbal usages.

86. In *Law and Theology*, pp. 21ff.

87. F. Dumermuth, 'Zur deuteronomischen Kulttheologie', *ZAW* 70 (1958), p. 63, cf. 69ff. (Bethel); von Rad, *Deuteronomy* (London: SCM Press, 1966), p. 94; *idem*, *Studies*, p. 38 (Bethel or Shiloh); O. Eissfeldt, 'Silo und Jerusalem', in *Congress Volume, Strasbourg 1956* (ed. J.A. Emerton *et al.*; VTSup, 4; Leiden: Brill,

In this case Jerusalem could be conceived as having taken over the
authority originally conferred by it on some predecessor. Such a view
was congenial to Noth's thesis regarding an amphictyony, which saw a
succession of places functioning in turn as the central sanctuary of that
institution. A variation on the idea of the formula having other referents
than Jerusalem was provided by A.C. Welch. He thought that, in its
original form, the formula may have referred to a number of different
places concurrently. He made a distinction, however, between the forms
found in Deut. 12.14 and 12.5. In the former, the phrase, 'in one of your
tribes' might be construed distributively, as 'in any of your tribes'. In
support of this he appealed, with Oestreicher, to a similar phrase in Deut.
23.17.[88] The latter case, however (Deut. 12.5), could not be so understood, but must refer to a single sanctuary. He agreed, despite his opposition to Wellhausen's general theory, that this passage must have its
context in Josiah's reform. For him too then, the formula came to refer
to Jerusalem, though it did not originally do so.

The possibilities aired here have been kept alive in more recent work.
Halpern's treatment of the altar-law has echoes of Welch, though he
rejects the latter's distributive interpretation of 12.14.[89] He finds an early
form of the law in Deuteronomy 16. The formula, as it occurs for
example in 16.2 (במקום אשר יבחר יהוה לשכן שמו שם) is capable of various
translations: 'a place—the place—any place...' The original formula,
therefore, was not an instrument of the centralizing reform at Jerusalem.
The use of the verb שכן in this formula he also finds significant, having
connotations of mobility. He recalls in this connection the theory of
J. Dus that the law originally referred to the ark of the covenant.[90]

Deuteronomy 12, however, changes this picture. There, an old
centralizing law (12.13-19), which had been the original preface to the
law-code, is augmented by further centralizing laws (12.20-28, 1-12).
Where the early law had used the unique form of the formula: 'the place
which the LORD will choose in one of your tribes', the later laws are
now characterized by the use of the verb שום for the placing of the name

1956), pp. 138-48 (Shiloh); H.H. Rowley, *Worship in Ancient Israel* (London:
SPCK), p. 106 (Shechem).
    88.   A.C. Welch, *The Code of Deuteronomy* (London: J. Clarke, 1924), p. 48;
T. Oestreicher, *Das Deuteronomische Grundgesetz* (Gütersloh: Mohn, 1923),
pp. 246ff.
    89.   Halpern, 'The Centralization-Formula', pp. 22-23.
    90.   Halpern, 'The Centralization-Formula', pp. 24-25, 34.

at the sanctuary. Deut. 12.5 actually completes the change of concept from the formula as it appears in Deuteronomy 16 by assimilating the שכן usage to that of שום.[91] With this change the idea of a mobile sanctuary is abolished, and the requirement to slaughter sacrificially at the sanctuary is now understood in terms of Josiah's reform, and the permanent claims of Jerusalem.

There are several obvious problems with Halpern's reconstruction. First, there is no satisfactory demonstration of the alleged transition from שכן forms to שום forms, with the attendant interpretation of an evolution towards a Josianic doctrine. The relative earliness of the former is affirmed on the basis on Deuteronomy 16. In Deuteronomy 12, however, *neither* verb appears in the putative early version (12.13-19), but only the unique form in v. 14. It is impossible, therefore, to trace a development of thought on this basis within Deuteronomy 12, or indeed to establish a clear difference in connotation between the verbs.[92]

Secondly, the argument rests on older literary-critical habits of thought about the composition of Deuteronomy 12 which cannot be sustained. These include the alternation of singular and plural address, and the belief that variations in the formula itself must be explained in terms of religious-historical evolution. The older analysis, furthermore, has no analogues anywhere in Deuteronomy. In fact the features of the chapter can be explained in literary and stylistic terms. Singular and plural address has increasingly been found unreliable as a means of identifying literary layers in Deuteronomy.[93] Variations in the formula can readily be regarded as stylistic. The alleged versions of the centralization-law, moreover, are not such; rather, there is a progression of thought in the chapter, and a carefully constructed balance of language and idea.[94]

Nevertheless Halpern has made an important observation about

---

91. A similar argument was made by G. Seitz, *Redaktionsgeschichtliche Studien zum Deuteronomium* (Stuttgart: Kohlhammer, 1971), pp. 212ff.

92. Seitz supposed that in the shortest form of the formula: 'the place which the LORD your God will choose', the addition 'to place (שכן) his name there' was understood even where omitted (*Redaktionsgeschichtliche Studien zum Deuteronomium*, p. 214). This, however, cannot be demonstrated.

93. See Lohfink, *Das Hauptgebot*, pp. 239ff.; Mayes, *Deuteronomy*, pp. 35-37; Braulik, *Mittel deuteronomischer Rhetorik*, pp. 146-50; cf. McConville, *Grace in the End*, pp. 36-39. Contrast, however, Preuss, *Deuteronomium*, pp. 95, 103; Mittmann, *Deuteronomium 1.1–6.3*.

94. I have tried to show this in detail in *Law and Theology*, pp. 58-67.

the meaning of the formula itself, namely that it does not determine a particular place. This is not to revert to the distributive view of Welch, for even in 12.14 the plain implication is that *one* place is meant.[95] The identity of the place is not at issue, however; indeed, the formula is consistent with a reference of the 'place' to several sanctuaries in succession. Halpern's point that the verb שכן has connotations of mobility has some force. I would prefer to argue from usage, however, and am more persuaded by the occurrence of the verb in Jer. 7.12 with reference to Shiloh. On the broader canvas of Deuteronomic and related literature the formula clearly has in fact been made to refer to a succession of sanctuaries.[96] Furthermore, there is nothing in the altar-law itself, in my view, in any of its forms in Deuteronomy, that is in tension with such an application in the Deuteronomic literature. Halpern's belief that 12.1-8 must be understood in relation to Josiah's centralization of the cult rests on other grounds than the syntax of the formula itself in 12.5 (grounds which we found inadequate).

I have argued elsewhere that the emphasis of the altar-law lies on the prerogative of Yahweh to choose the place where he should be worshipped, as part of Deuteronomy's affirmation of his rights, as opposed to the claims of other gods, in every aspect of the life of Israel.[97] In that context I took the view that Deuteronomy 12 required a central sanctuary, while not precluding other legitimate ones, though I saw as a corollary that the formula could indeed have applied to a succession of central sanctuaries.[98] The chief difficulty for the idea of a central sanctuary as opposed to a sole one is the phrase 'out of all your tribes' in 12.5, which seems more exclusive than the phrase 'in one of your tribes' (12.14). This was what led Welch to accept that 12.1-8 was a genuine centralizing law. For this reason I am no longer convinced that the idea of a central sanctuary does best justice to the use of the formula in Deuteronomy 12. Nor do I think that there is an important difference between the various forms of the formula in the book. Throughout the law-code it most naturally refers to a single place, but its requirement may be met in a number of places in succession. The ceremony prescribed for Shechem in Deuteronomy 27, furthermore,

---

95. Halpern, 'The Centralization-Formula', p. 35.

96. See above, on the Old Testament's application of the formula.

97. McConville, *Law and Theology*, pp. 29-35.

98. McConville, *Law and Theology*, pp. 28-29; cf. G.J. Wenham, 'Deuteronomy and the Central Sanctuary', *TynBul* 22 (1971), pp. 103-18.

may readily be understood in this connection. The view taken here has also been advocated recently by J.J. Niehaus.[99]

I have dealt so far with the elements of the altar-law formula as if they were separate topics for interpretation. Clearly, however, it is important to ask whether there is a rationale which binds them into a coherent whole. This has not been an easy question for the traditional interpretations, as we have seen. Thus, when name theology was taken as a means of asserting the transcendence and spirituality of God over against a sacral idea of him, it was hard to account satisfactorily for the phrase 'before the LORD', which seemed to affirm his real presence at the sanctuary. Similarly the belief that the place formula served the claims of a particular sanctuary suited a sacral theology, but could accommodate the attendant belief in a spiritualizing Deuteronomy only by means of a notion of compromise between competing points of view. This discussion admittedly is wider than the interpretation of the altar-law itself. Nevertheless that law plays a key part in it, especially because, as we have seen, other features of Deuteronomy, such as the law of the king, are somewhat enigmatic when pressed to yield information on Deuteronomy's ideology. I believe that many of the difficulties we have observed arise because a fixed idea about one or another element in the formula has been allowed to dominate over the understanding of it as a whole.

We have seen that the name of Yahweh in Deuteronomy (and related literature) is not a device to preserve the transcendence of Yahweh; rather, it serves, more subtly, to affirm both his transcendence and his presence, as part of an explication of his character. The phrase 'before the LORD' should not be evacuated of its plain meaning; it assumes that Yahweh may truly be met at the sanctuary. This is the purpose of meeting God at the 'place' which he will choose.

Thus far the balance seems to shift away from the spiritualizing, demythologizing view of Deuteronomy towards a more sacral one. All elements in the formula insist on Yahweh's presence at the sanctuary, though the name theology also guards his transcendence. However, the relationship between presence and transcendence is actually more firmly grounded than in the name element alone. There are two reasons for thinking so.

The first arises from our consideration of the place formula. Not only

99. J.J. Niehaus, 'The Central Sanctuary: Where and When?', *TynBul* 43.1 (1992), pp. 3-30.

is the sanctuary not named, but the formula does not even have the force of requiring one sanctuary for all time. This militates against the view that the formula is an apologia for a particular sanctuary. Since that is so, the idea that the formula carries with it in some degree the sacral conceptions of Zion theology, with their specific stress on Yahweh's presence in Zion, has little cogency.

The second reason for finding a balance between presence and transcendence in the altar-law concerns the element of Yahweh's choice. I did not consider it separately above because in itself it has not been a controversial topic in the interpretation of the formula. The force of it, however, has in my view generally been underestimated. Where the formula has been read as an affirmation of the claims of Jerusalem, then the element of Yahweh's choice has been interpreted accordingly, namely, as part of the apologia for Jerusalem. Where the identity of the place is genuinely not an issue, however, then the importance of Yahweh's choice appears more clearly. It functions simply to affirm his rights in respect of Israel's worship. As such it fits well with the Deuteronomic insistence on his sovereignty, and indeed 'choice' itself constitutes a significant motif in Deuteronomy in that sense.[100] Yahweh's choice of an unnamed place has the effect of asserting his freedom in respect of that place. (The motif of choice has a similar effect in relation to the king, Deut. 17.14-20; there it functions to retain Yahweh's rights, and incidentally the primacy of Torah in Israel.) In relation to the 'place' element in the formula, therefore, there is an analogy with the element of the name. In both cases a delicate balance is maintained between the giving of God's presence and the retaining of his freedom or independence.

It seems to me, therefore, that attempts to understand the altar-law have suffered from the imposition of false categories and polarizations. It is neither an affirmation of the sacral over against the spiritual, nor the reverse, nor a deliberate middle way between the two. Rather, it is Deuteronomy's distinctive way of affirming the actual presence of Yahweh among his people, which nevertheless allows him to assert his own character. The choice of a place is not the end of a story, for Yahweh will not be bound to one place for ever. The openness of the formula, with its resistance to the identification of a 'place', is essential to the ideology that it embodies. That ideology is to be understood in terms of Yahweh's relationship with his people in a covenantal history,

100. Cf. my *Law and Theology*, pp. 30-32.

and it characterizes Deuteronomy in a profound way.

The proposed interpretation is different, I think, from all the main current views of Deuteronomy. It stands against the compromise views of Clements and others, and also the demythologizing theory of Weinfeld. It differs most, perhaps, from Halpern's 'statist' interpretation, which tries to harmonize spiritual and sacral concepts in a Jerusalem-centred reform of state and cult. In Halpern's view, Deuteronomy attempts to proclaim the consummation of Israel's history in the Josianic state. In mine, it does precisely the opposite. History with Israel's God cannot end in an institution dedicated to the *status quo*.

It is interesting to notice at this stage a certain congruence between our findings about the meaning of the altar-law and the earliest interpretations of it, which we noticed above. The Deuteronomic historian saw the fulfilment of the command enshrined in the altar-law in a succession of actual cultic places. Jeremiah made a point of this succession when he insisted that the fulfilment of the promise implied in the altar-law in a given place constituted no permanent guarantee of God's presence in that place in particular. Many of the later Jewish writings, as we saw, adopted in some sense DtH's 'Shiloh' interpretation. The fact that the chosen place is actually Jerusalem for the later biblical writers, as well as the post-biblical Jewish ones, does not contradict this point. For they too know that Jerusalem can fall under judgment. The identity of the place is not intrinsically at issue. Rather it is the nature of the presence of God, and the rationale behind his remaining at any time with his people.

### 3. The 'Chosen Place' in Deuteronomic Context

The next stage of our study tries to put the altar-law in the context of related themes in Deuteronomy. It is our belief that this involves a consideration of the themes of time and place in the book, since those themes arise from the formula itself, and its immediate context: '*When* you cross the Jordan (11.31)...you shall seek the *place*...' (12.5).[101] The present argument therefore builds essentially on G. Millar's study in the present volume on the themes of time and place in the 'framework' of Deuteronomy. The main points established there were the following: that the motifs of 'journey' and history were intimately connected with the Deuteronomic parenesis; that the encounter between God and Israel at

---

101. On the rhetorical connections between the closing verses of ch. 11 and the beginning of ch. 12, see Lohfink, e.g. '*Huqqim Umishpatim*', p. 22.

Moab was conceived as a new moment of decision on the models of previous such encounters, especially at Kadesh and at Horeb; that the geography of Deuteronomy had a moral/religious contour, in the sense that progress and regress were measures of covenant faithfulness (the situation at the end of Deuteronomy 1 is one of 'Anti-Exodus'); that the boundaries between the moments of encounter even appeared to break down, as when the Horeb generation, though it can be distinguished from that of Moab in Deuteronomy 1–3, is effectively identified with it in Deuteronomy 5–11. This is intended to stress the solidarity of Israel, in the interests of the thesis that it is the same covenant people that once again chooses for or against the covenant. Israel's moral life is characterized by the succession of failure and further opportunity. It is plain that the concept of Israel's covenant life draws heavily on the ideas of time and place. Geographical or 'journey' motifs intersect with temporal ones; Israel is always 'on the move', both literally and spiritually.

*Present and Future in the Code*
It is now time to ask whether the same motifs also play a role in the 'code' of Deuteronomy (Deut. 12–26), as a prelude to a discussion of the meaning of the altar-law. Certain *prima facie* features suggest that they do. There is a pervading sense of the future as opposed to the now. The point is highlighted, enigmatically, in 12.8-9: 'You shall not act as we are acting here today... for you have not come into the rest and the possession that the LORD your God is giving you'. The idea of 'going over' into the land is ubiquitous.

The command to 'go over' is interwoven with the promise that at a future time the people would enjoy rest from their enemies (12.10, cf. 2 Sam. 7.1). This promise belongs closely with the motif of expulsion of the peoples that are currently in the land. The notion of displacement, significantly, opens the section of laws (12.2-4), and thus picks up the note that was struck in chs. 1–3, namely the link between faithfulness, progress and overcoming the enemy, as well as the closely related passage in 7.1-5. The point echoes the sense of progression from Transjordan to the land west of Jordan in Deuteronomy 1–3.

In common with that section of the book too, however, is a sense that the arriving is only part of something that continues. Indeed arriving and dispossessing carry dangers with them, for there might yet be temptations to be ensnared by other gods. This danger lies behind the command in 12.29-31, which thus not merely echoes 12.2-4, with which it forms an *inclusio*, but also marks an advance upon it in terms of its temporal perspective. The thought is not far from that of Deuteronomy 8, with its sense of the danger of 'arrival', there in terms of satiety. The sequel of ch. 12, furthermore, envisages a future time, or times, when the people might be led astray by false prophets to other gods (13.2-19). All three temporal perspectives, past, present and future, are here: a reminder of the deliverance from Egypt (vv. 6, 11), a reference to the commands that are being given 'today' (v. 19), and a sense of a future that stretches out indefinitely (the town devoted to destruction shall be a 'perpetual ruin, never to be rebuilt', v. 17). Possession of land lays upon Israel a perpetual obligation to be faithful. This is sometimes explicitly conceived in terms of succeeding generations (12.28). The law of the king similarly envisages the rule not of an individual only but of a dynasty (17.20). In the same chapter, the office of judge is portrayed in terms of an ongoing history (17.9).

In other texts, specific future developments are envisaged, as in 12.20: 'When the LORD your God enlarges your territory, as he has promised you'. The context here is the permission to eat meat away from the 'chosen place', with certain conditions attached. The accompanying phrase כי תאוה נפשך (cf. בכל אות נפשך, vv. 15, 20) can be read as an iterative future ('whenever', NRSV), suggesting in its own way an ongoing life in the land.

A similar perspective to that in the passage just quoted, and forging a connection between framework and code, occurs in the resumption in 19.1-10 of the motif of cities of refuge, initiated in 4.41-43. In the earlier passage the cities were located in Transjordan only. Now three are added in the west, with the provision that yet three more may be added 'When the LORD enlarges your territory' (vv. 8-9).

It is clear from the foregoing that the code distinguishes between the present time and the future. Yet as with the framework it can also conceive of Israel as essentially a unity transcending the generations. This, I think, is a function of the use of the singular form of second-person address, associated further with the idea of brotherhood. The connection is striking in ch. 17, where the legal provisions are clearly addressed to Israel as a body politic, in its plurality and diversity, where the idea of brotherhood is invoked to qualify the character of the kingship (v. 20), and where the provisions are enacted for the generations to come. In its capacity, therefore, both to distinguish between the generations and to

conceive of Israel as a single entity, the code shares an important feature
with the framework.

### The View of the Future in Deuteronomy 12–26

From the foregoing inevitably arises the question, what kind of future
the code of Deuteronomy envisages for Israel, and how that vision
relates to possession of the land. An important stimulus to this question
has been given by N. Lohfink. In a study of the expression חקים ומשפטים
he argues that in the final redaction of Deuteronomy, the law-code
applies only to the time of Israel's occupation of the land. He claims to
see a development in the usage of the expression with the result that two
different concepts coexist in the book. The first, found in 5.31 and
6.1,[102] is an appositional use, where the phrase simply refers to the laws
being propounded by Moses. This use corresponds to the concept of ch.
5, namely that the words of Moses take on equal authority with laws
already received at Horeb. On this view of חקים ומשפטים the phrase refers
to all laws promulgated by a duly designated authority.[103]

The second use of the expression arises in conjunction with its adoption as a structural marker of the main sections of the book, chs. 5–11
and 12–26. That process was not itself simple, for Lohfink detects a
distinction between the scope of the phrase in 6.1 and 12.1; the former
understands it to include the Decalogue and the whole *Hauptgebot*,
whereas the latter applies it exclusively to the laws of chs. 12–26. This
view of the phrase's meaning prevailed in the final redaction (he
interprets 5.1 and 11.32 accordingly).[104] The corollary of this is that the
laws of 12–26 are understood in the redaction to be valid only for the
period when Israel occupies the land. This is plain from the terms of 12.1
itself, Lohfink argues, because of the phrases 'in the land', and 'all the
days that you live upon the earth' (where the latter term, אדמה, is taken
as a synonym of ארץ).[105]

This view contrasts with that found in 5.29, 31, where the laws are

---

102. He argues on text-critical grounds that the term's asyndetic relationship with
the noun המצוה, as in 6.1, is primary; contrast 5.31; N. Lohfink, '*Huqqim
Umishpatim*', pp. 1-2.

103. Lohfink, '*Huqqim Umishpatim*', pp. 7-8.

104. Lohfink, '*Huqqim Umishpatim*', pp. 17-18.

105. Lohfink, '*Huqqim Umishpatim*', p. 23, for the synonymity of אדמה and ארץ,
following Plöger, *Deuteronomium*, pp. 121-29. Contrast L. Rost, 'Die Bezeichnungen
für Land und Volk', in *Das kleine Credo und andere Studien zum Alten Testament*
(Heidelberg: Quelle & Meyer, 1934), pp. 76-101 (77).

seen as valid for all time. The same concept undergirds 6.1-2, which
knows a solidarity of Israel in all generations. Deut. 12.1, however, may
consciously distance itself from that perception.[106] In its view
(presumably deriving from the *Golah*, only the Decalogue and the
*Hauptgebot* have perpetual validity.[107]

Lohfink has thus put a question to the thesis that the framework and
the code exhibit the same basic attitude to the future of Israel, as I have
begun to argue above. His reconstruction, however, has certain weaknesses. For example, the alleged development in the usage of the phrase
חקים ומשפטים is itself open to question. Further, the textual evidence on
the relative primacy of the asyndetic and syndetic usages of the phrase is
at best mixed,[108] and the separation of the two words by ומצותיו in 26.17
suggests the pairing is not fully explained in terms of apposition. (Here I
think Braulik is right, against both Lohfink and Plöger. He believes that
the law, expressed by the phrase חקים ומשפטים, refers to Deut. 5–26, that
is, not only the code but also the parenesis.)[109]

There are more fundamental objections, however, to the dichotomy
which Lohfink claims to find within Deuteronomy's statements about
the law and the land. Most importantly, the equation of ארץ and אדמה
needs at least to be qualified. It is true that the terms are sometimes
synonymous, as in 11.8-9; 4.38, 40, where both refer to the land of
Canaan, as Plöger argued.[110] Plöger admitted, however, that such an
equation might have levelled previous nuances of the terms, and others
have insisted that they are in fact distinguishable in Deuteronomy.
G. Minette de Tillesse, for example, thought that אדמה had a more
general meaning than 'promised land' in certain texts.[111]

In fact both terms have a complex semantic range in the book. Each
can refer to the promised land (as we have noticed), and does so
frequently. Equally, however, each is sometimes correctly translated
'earth'. In the case of ארץ, the reference is typically to the whole earth
(as opposed to the heavens; 3.24; 4.39). אדמה, on the other hand, often

---

106. Lohfink, '*Huqqim Umishpatim*', pp. 24-25.

107. Lohfink, '*Huqqim Umishpatim*', p. 26.

108. As Lohfink shows, the LXX and SamP represent opposite positions, with MT
mediating; '*Huqqim Umishpatim*', p. 2.

109. Braulik, 'Ausdrücke für Gesetz', pp. 61-62.

110. Plöger, *Deuteronomium*, p. 128.

111. E.g. Minette de Tillesse, 'Sections "Vous"', p. 53 n. 1; cf. Rost,
*Bezeichnungen*, p. 77.

connotes 'earth' as fruitful ground (26.2, 10). This distinction is not thoroughgoing. There are cases, for example, where ארץ verges on the idea of fruitful land, as in 1.25 (מפרי הארץ). Here, however, the focus of the passage is on the promised land, the context being the journey towards that land; the fruit of the 'earth', therefore, is specifically of the promised 'land'. In 26.2aα, in contrast, the focus (of אדמה) is on the regular fruitfulness of the ground. Here, indeed, the idea of 'promised land' is not far away, as the following phrase shows (v. 2aβ). However, that very contrast within the verse illustrates the point that the two words have a perceptibly different focus. An analogous distinction between the two words is found in 4.17-18 (where ארץ refers to the whole earth, and אדמה to the 'ground').

In these cases, of course, the distinctions are brought out by the context. The vocabulary is, in fact, capable of being used in diverse ways. In 28.11, for example, the word אדמה is used twice within the space of three words in the different senses 'ground' and (promised) 'land'. This repetition, however, is simply a function of Deuteronomy's varied rhetoric, which plays here on the natural intimacy between the ideas of fruitful land and promised land in the book's theology.

It is just such nuances, however, that Lohfink does not recognize when he insists that the terms are merely synonymous. (The point may be further reinforced by the fact that אדמה cannot refer to other 'lands', such as Egypt, or to the whole earth.) The discussion of the terms ארץ and אדמה opens up dimensions of the theology of Deuteronomy which are thus missed. In contrast to Lohfink, it is our contention that the view of law and land is similar in the code to that in the framework. On Lohfink's view, the law only applies when the people are in the land. It is true in one sense that law-keeping and land-occupation are regarded as co-extensive. However, Lohfink's thesis robs Deuteronomy of the tension that is built into its conception. The point is not that the law is relevant only to the time in the land, then becomes inoperative; rather, it is imperative to obey the law, in covenant faithfulness, in order to remain in the land, in relationship with God. Deuteronomy always envisages life in the land, and always calls Israel to 'enter' it.

However, this relationship between land and life requires some elaboration. In Deuteronomy, land is not just a place, but an arena of life, the life of Israel in covenant relationship with God. That life is rich; not only the earth, but also flocks and herds and even the people themselves will be fruitful (7.13-15; cf. 12.6-7, 17, 20-21). Land and full life are inseparable in this conception; possession and enjoyment are facets of the same whole, as we see from the juxtaposition of 'exodus–conquest' statements with wealth motifs (6.10-11, 12; 8.12-13, 14-16). The idea of life is never separated from that of the land in Deuteronomy. Possession of the land is not for one generation only, but continues for indefinite generations (12.28). Even when Deuteronomy faces the fact of exile as the consequence of covenant-breach (28.68) it sees the healing of that breach in terms of a return to the land. And this return is not only a new exodus and conquest, but it issues in a new prosperity and fruitfulness, once again reaching into the future (30.1-10; note vv. 3-5, 9). This passage has sometimes been thought post-Deuteronomistic. But it is entirely 'Deuteronomic' in its fusion of land and life (cf. vv. 15-16).

The concept of full life in the land brings a certain tension, however, namely between the actual and the ideal. The ideal view is reflected in certain portrayals of the wealth of the land which verge on the paradisal (in the framework, 8.7-10, cf. 6.10-11; in the code, 12.12; 14.28-29). In contrast, both framework and code know of the possibility that life may not always live up to this. (The framework has built the possibility of non-possession into its parenesis; the law-code provides for cases of debt and slavery. The contrast between two phrases in ch. 15 is striking: 'But there will be no poor among you', v. 4; and 'For the poor will never cease out of the land', v. 11.)

Some scholars have described Deuteronomy's view of the future as 'eschatological' because of this tension. Plöger thinks of the land as a 'gift of salvation' (*Heilsgabe*) that is both 'present' and 'eschatological'.[112] The land has an eschatological character because it is received in fulfilment of a promise, the oath to the patriarchs. The status of the land as gift means that Israel does not enjoy it by right.[113] In this sense, actual enjoyment of the land is never an end in itself. The concept of history (expressed according to Plöger in the cult) consists in a perpetual succession of promise–fulfilment–promise. 'Die Verheissung behält trotz ihrer zeitweisen präsentischen Erfüllung eschatologischen Charakter.'[114]

The term 'eschatology' itself may raise more questions than it answers. Nevertheless Plöger's use of it is an attempt to do justice to

---

112. Plöger, *Deuteronomium*, p. 61.

113. Plöger, *Deuteronomium*, pp. 78-79.

114. Plöger, *Deuteronomium*, p. 82 ('The promise retains, despite its fulfilment in the present from time to time, its eschatological character').

what may be called the bifocal character of Deuteronomy, both in the framework and the code, that is, its assertion both of the fulfilment of the land promise in the conquest under Joshua and its understanding that the same promise remains perpetually to be appropriated.

The relationship, finally, between the terms ארץ and אדמה may be understood in the context of this Deuteronomic conception. I have suggested above that there is a perceptible tendency for the former to be used to connote the promised land, while the latter is more readily used for arable ground, the basis of life and fruitfulness. The two ideas, however, are closely related in Deuteronomic theology. The land is the place where God's chosen people may enjoy the good things of the earth which he has made. The terms in question can trade on each other in a variety of ways in order to bring out this close association. This is the best way to understand them in Deut. 12.1. Law-keeping in the land is God's appointed way for Israel to have life on the earth. The same is true of 26.2. The two passages, incidentally, occupying crucial positions at the beginning and end of the law-code, as Lohfink has observed, form a chiasmus in their use of the two terms:

> 'Be careful to do (the commandments) in the land (הארץ) which the
>   LORD...has given you...
> all the days that you live upon the earth (האדמה) (12.1).

> You shall take some of all the first of the fruit of the ground (האדמה),
>   which you harvest from your land (מארצך) that the LORD your God gives
>       you (26.2).

This feature may hint at a correspondence between the two passages. I think, however, that they are not mere structural markers, but also express the view of the land outlined in the foregoing. That is to say, it is the place where, in actuality, Israel is to enter into God's purposes and blessings. Those purposes, however, cannot be circumscribed by the actual possession of the land at any given time.

### *Place* (מקום) *in Deuteronomy 12–26*

Our consideration of the idea of the land in the foregoing was intended to sketch the broad context of the formula concerning the chosen place in the lawcode. The next stage of the argument is to examine the use of the term המקום itself.

In the book of Deuteronomy the noun המקום has a number of referents. These are (i) Moab (1.31; 9.7; 11.5; 29.6); (ii) places to camp *en route* to the land (1.33); (iii) places in the land (11.24; 21.19); (iv) the chosen place of worship (12.5 etc.); (v) false places of worship (12.2; 12.13?); (vi) the promised land itself (26.9? 12.3?). This general observation is not surprising in view of what we have seen of the role of changes of place in the book. However, it provides *prima facie* evidence that the altar-law may not be an isolated feature of Deuteronomy, but part of a larger tendency in the book. There are reasons to suppose that this is so.

First, there is a clear progression of 'places' in the transition from ch. 11 to ch. 12. In 11.5, place refers to Moab; in 11.24 the reference is to every place within the land, which the people will subdue. The focus in the opening verses of ch. 12 then switches to sanctuaries, both the false ones of the peoples of the land, and that which, in contrast, Yahweh will choose for his people. Yet there is some ambiguity here as between 'place' as sanctuary, and 'place' as land. This emerges from v. 3. The passage continues the command of v. 2 to eradicate Ba'al worship from sanctuaries (places) in the land, and concludes: '(you shall) destroy their name out of that place'. This last occurrence does not refer logically to the sanctuaries, since one would expect a plural. It is better to take it of the land; in destroying the places of false worship, the names of the false gods are removed from the whole land. There is, of course, an interplay between the two uses of the noun, corresponding to a close connection in concept between sanctuary and land. Nevertheless, it is significant that the command concerning the altar-law is bound into the overarching concept of 'place' in the book. The land is a place in a succession of places; the chosen place of worship stands in relationship to the land, and is therefore subordinate to the general tendency of the motif of place in the book.

The correlation of land and chosen place is also indicated by 26.9. The phrase 'this place' (המקום הזה) could in that text refer either to the sanctuary (since the context is a confession made there) or to the land. The latter is the more natural interpretation, because the confession concerns the exodus from Egypt and entry into the land, and because of the parallelism with 'this land' (הארץ הזאת) in the following phrase. (The structure of 26.9-10, then, parallels that of chs. 1–11, 12–26; that is, first it speaks of the bringing of Israel to the land, then it evokes the proper response of Israel by bringing offerings to the sanctuary.[115]) Nevertheless, here too there may be some intended ambiguity, suggesting a close

115. For this relationship between structure and framework and law-code, see my *Law and Theology*, pp. 33-36.

connection between sanctuary and land.

The point of the connection between land and sanctuary in chs. 12 and 26 is twofold. First, it stresses the importance of right worship for the continuance of the covenant, and therefore for possession of the land. Secondly, the altar-law participates in the provisionality of 'places' in Deuteronomy.

It may be added that the place motif overlaps with that of time. In 11.5, Moses addresses the people who have come to 'this place' (= Moab), in the way which is typical of chs. 5–11, namely, identifying the Moab generation with that which came out of Egypt. An effect of this is to assert the essential unity of Israel in all generations, and the need to re-enact the covenant perpetually. In this context, no single generation is permitted absolute significance. Similarly, no place has such significance; Moab is clearly no more than a place 'on the way'. By the same token, however, the phrase 'this place' in 11.5 becomes ambiguous. If the Mosaic address is framed in such a way as to address each succeeding generation, then the allusion to 'this place' is subject also to that concept. When each generation stands again at the moment of the making of the covenant, then it does so in its own place. The 'place' in 11.5 thus opens on to a future in which 'places' are essentially provisional.

## *The 'Chosen Place' in Context: Conclusions*

It will be apparent that the broad contextual considerations which we have adduced support the interpretation which we offered earlier of the altar-law itself, namely that the terms of the altar-law could be met in a succession of actual places. If the language of 'place' in Deut. 12.1-5 is carefully interwoven with the theme in the wider context of the book, then the idea of a chosen place of worship is less concerned with identifying and supporting the claims of a sanctuary than with laying claim to the allegiance of Israel in worship, within a covenantal context, in which particular historical situations are subject to change. We are now in a position to take our argument further, however, by asking whether the altar-law makes its own distinctive contribution to the theology of time and place in Deuteronomy.

## 4. *Deuteronomy 12: Transcendence, Immanence and Contingency*

We have argued that the rhetoric of Deuteronomy, both in the parenesis and in the laws, aims to affirm the validity of the covenant from time to time and from place to place. There are analogies between the covenants at Horeb and in Moab, and between Moab and the continuing life of Israel in the land. These analogies are at the heart of the thinking of Deuteronomy: the people is always confronted again with the need to be faithful to the covenant now. The theological significance of these points may be explored further, however. Plainly, that significance is in terms of Deuteronomy's theology of God's presence, and this is illuminated, I believe, by the ideas of transcendence and immanence.

I have laid the foundations above of an understanding of Deuteronomy's theology of the divine presence. There I argued that its use of the divine 'name' did not imply the non-presence of God at the sanctuary (*contra* von Rad and others). On the contrary, Deuteronomy strongly affirmed the actual presence of God when it dealt with encounters between him and Israel. It follows, therefore, that we have identified two tendencies in Deuteronomy which at first sight seem paradoxical: on the one hand God is not uniquely associated with one place in particular; on the other, his real presence in 'places' is strongly affirmed.

The paradox here may be expressed in terms of transcendence and immanence. I have used this language in our discussion above of the nature of the divine presence in Deuteronomy. In his interpretation of Deut. 4.36, I. Wilson showed that that passage held together the dwelling of God in heaven and his actual presence on earth.[116] It seems to me that the theology of presence in that chapter helps illuminate the altar-law in ch. 12.

The relevance of Deuteronomy 4 to a study of Deuteronomy 12 may be maintained in general from the argument hitherto, in which I have tried to show the continuity between the parenesis and the law-code on the topic of time and place. G. Millar has shown in this volume that Deuteronomy 4 is integrated into the developing argument of chs. 1–11, by reason of its treatment of the theme of the law (especially the phrase חקים ומשפטים). The chapter is also important, however, for its under-standing of the divine presence. As we shall see, the two topics (law and presence) are related.

As Millar has pointed out, scholarship is divided on whether the chapter is a unity. The question is important, because on it turns the essential theological character of Deuteronomy 4. Von Rad observed what he thought was a disharmony in the chapter between the themes

of law and image prohibition.[117] This observation has now gained
further development in the study of D. Knapp. Knapp finds different literary layers in the chapter. Its kernel consists of vv. 1-4, 9-14, whose
central interest is the law. (These verses were augmented at a later date
by vv. 5-8, which see the Torah as that which fundamentally distinguished Israel from the nations).[118] The other major section of the
chapter, vv. 15-28, differs crucially from the first, because it has a quite
different interest, namely that of 'form', and the prohibition of images.
In Knapp's view, vv. 15-28 latch on to the 'minor' motif of form in
v. 12, and develop it. Like the first section, this passage knows the decalogue, but has focused on the one aspect of it which it sees as crucial.[119]
Finally, 4.29-40 lacks any interest in images, and pursues a quite different set of concerns.[120] Knapp concludes that the central concern of
the chapter is the theme established in vv. 1-14, namely that of law. The
chapter functions to introduce the theme of law that is taken up in the
ensuing chapters (5–11). It is also familiar with chs. 12–26, which it
therefore (presumably) understands primarily as law.[121] The themes of
'law' and 'form' are essentially different; image prohibition is not the
real interest of the chapter.[122]

In my view, Knapp has forced apart the themes of 'law' and 'form'
quite unduly. The giving of law is clearly associated with the presence of
God in v. 10, and it is arbitrary to declare the motif of form 'minor' in
v. 12. (The same association of ideas occurs, incidentally, in 9.10-15, 18.)
In fact, the interconnection of the two themes is highly important for the
theology of ch. 4, and it as at this level that Knapp's analysis must be
challenged.

The underlying concern of the chapter is God's transcendence and
immanence and the relationship between these. That is, how is it that
God, who is not contained within the world, may yet be near to Israel?
The theme is aired most clearly in vv. 32-40, where it is signalled by the
pairing of 'earth' (הארץ) and 'heaven' in v. 32. Verses 33 and 36 contain
what Knapp saw as a contradiction, because in the former God speaks

117. Von Rad, *Deuteronomy*, pp. 49-50.

118. Knapp, *Deuteronomium 4*, pp. 30-35, 66-67.

119. Knapp, *Deuteronomium 4*, pp. 30-31, 69. Deut. 4.16b-17, incidentally, he
sees as a secondary expansion within vv. 15-18; 36.

120. Knapp, *Deuteronomium 4*, p. 39.

121. Knapp, *Deuteronomium 4*, pp. 56, 88.

122. Knapp, *Deuteronomium 4*, pp. 30-31, 69, 88.

out of the fire on Horeb, while in the latter he speaks from heaven.[123] It is clear, however, that the passage as a whole intends to allow these statements to stand together (if v. 36b were an attempt to smooth a contradiction it would be extremely inept). The thought is not new in itself.[124] Exodus knew both that Yahweh was in heaven (20.22) and that he was actually present on Mt Sinai (24.17). Deuteronomy's contribution (as Weinfeld notes) is to synthesize these spatial aspects of his presence.[125] And v. 36 itself contains the nub of the point: God is both in heaven and with his people on earth. The issue raised here is *how* this can be so, and in articulating this the chapter carefully guards the transcendence aspect.

The characteristic way in which it does this is in the distinction between hearing and seeing (v. 12b); the people at Horeb heard a voice, but saw no form. The presence of God among his people is thus closely bound to the words spoken, and indeed to the Ten Commandments (4.13). Presence thus envisaged is opposed to presence as localized in an image; the appearance of no form at Horeb is the ground for the prohibition of images (vv. 15-18; cf. Exod. 20.22-23 for the same logic).

Finally, Yahweh's uniqueness is stressed; no other God has revealed himself in such a way (v. 33;—notice, incidentally, how the 'hearing' motif here modifies a thought more generally associated with seeing), or acted thus on behalf of his people (v. 34).

Yet God is not only in heaven but also on earth. The immanence of God is also strongly stated in Deuteronomy 4, actually even before the first development of its opposite. This is in the idea of Yahweh's 'nearness' to his people (v. 7). He has come close at Horeb; the people stand 'before' him (v. 10); they in turn are 'near' him (v. 11). The mountain (or the fire on it?) is the place at which the transcendent God meets the earth and is among his people. The classic statement of this paradox is in v. 36 (cf. also v. 39).

It will be clear by now why the two topics of law and form cannot be separated in the thought of the chapter. The law is closely connected with the idea of God's nearness in the chapter (vv. 7-8). This is a quite distinctive contribution to the idea of divine immanence, for it ties it firmly to covenantal law and the call to Israel to remain faithful. Such a concept of immanence stands over against the localization of the deity as

---

123. Knapp, *Deuteronomium 4*, pp. 106-107.
124. It is arguably already in Egypt and Canaan.
125. M. Weinfeld, *Deuteronomy 1–11* (AB; New York: Doubleday, 1991), p. 213.

in an image. The absence of a visible form at Horeb and the prohibition of images therefore dovetails with the chapter's understanding of God's presence, and safeguards in its own way the freedom of God from being bound into the created order.

It will be evident how the understanding of the presence of God just outlined corresponds to the motifs of time and place which we have been discussing. With the idea of God's immanence, bound to that of covenant, goes a certain particularity. The revelation of (the unique) Yahweh is to a specific, unique people (vv. 6-8, 33-34). The event at Horeb is a particular event in time and space. Moreover, bounds are carefully set around this people. Distinct from other nations, they are to occupy a particular land at a given time.

It is at this point that the relevance of the discussion to the themes of time and space emerges. Deuteronomy 4 shows an awareness of Israel relative to other times and places. As to 'space', it is set in the world of nations (vv. 6-8). The language of creation, 'man upon the earth' (v. 32), sets Israel within a history of the world, linking time and space dimensions. The time frame itself is very evident, extending as it does from the creation through the exodus from Egypt (vv. 34, 37), and the present time ('And now', v. 1) to future covenant unfaithfulness and exile (vv. 25-28), and finally repentance and restoration (vv. 29-31). The time line is one of promise–fulfilment (in terms of both blessing and judgment, vv. 26-31); the context of it is the promise made to the patriarchs, and the mercy of God (v. 31). In the covenant history, Yahweh knows Israel in different circumstances, and in changing places.[126]

Yahweh's choice of Israel, therefore, is contingent—both in the sense that history moves on, and that all depends on Israel's faithfulness to the covenant. This contingency follows necessarily from the 'immanence' side of the transcendence–immanence polarity. The election of Israel does not lose sight of other places (nations) or other times. The land which becomes Israel's inheritance will be held in a certain tension arising from this. It may, indeed will, be lost—but may also be regained.

---

126. Cf. the comment of I. Seeligmann that a sense of time—especially the distinction between the Horeb generation and the next—is of the essence of Deuteronomy: 'Erkenntnis Gottes und historisches Bewusstsein im alten Israel', in *Beiträge zur Alttestamentlichen Theologie* (FS W. Zimmerli; ed. H. Donner, R. Hanhart and R. Smend; Göttingen: Vandenhoeck & Ruprecht, 1977), p. 444. He associates the idea of knowing God by hearing the word with the rise of historical consciousnes in Israel.

Thus, in relation to his immanent (covenantal) presence in the world, Yahweh retains his freedom—a function of his transcendence.[127] In the Deuteronomic story, Israel goes to a land from which it will be removed. The paradox is this: Yahweh enters a relationship with a people, Israel, which requires an actual location in space and time; yet Yahweh is not bound by any necessity to that people, nor to any one place.

## Analogies between Deuteronomy 4 and Deuteronomy 12

It remains to apply the results of our study so far to the interpretation of the altar-law, first by drawing attention to similarities between Deuteronomy 4 and Deuteronomy 12. In doing so, we build on the interpretation of Deut. 12.1-5 offered above. There I argued that both the name theology of the law-code and the expression 'before the LORD' indicated a real presence of God at the sanctuary. I also suggested, in the context of a survey of past interpretation, that the 'place' itself could refer to a number of different sanctuaries in succession.

In bringing to bear our interpretation of ch. 4 we can fill out that interpretation. There are, I think, certain evident similarities between the chapters. The first concerns Torah-keeping. Each chapter opens with the exhortation to keep the commandments, and makes of this a prerequisite of life in the land (4.1; 12.1). In the same connection is the command to teach succeeding generations, that they too might have long life in the land (4.40; 12.28). And length of days itself is important in this connection, again in both chapters (4.10, 40; 12.28). These connections establish a certain *prima facie* similarity of interest between the two texts.

More important for our purposes are the connections between the ideas surrounding the presence of Yahweh among his people in the two places. In each, the people is depicted as standing 'before the LORD', at Horeb (4.10), and at the chosen 'place' (12.7). In ch. 12 as in ch. 4, I think, the ideas of transcendence and immanence help the interpretation. Yahweh's transcendence is expressed in the idea of his choice of the place, a function of his freedom. (As we have already observed, the idea of Yahweh's choice is an important means in Deuteronomy of expressing that freedom: 7.6; 17.15; 18.5).

The divine immanence, on the other hand, is caught in the idea of the chosen place itself, which is the focus of the meeting between Yahweh and people in their regular life of worship—and where they actually

---

127. On transcendence and freedom, see K. Barth, *Church Dogmatics*, II.1 (Edinburgh: T. & T. Clark, 1957), p. 302.

stand 'before the LORD'. Therefore, as Yahweh once met Israel at Horeb—in heaven yet presenced on earth among them in a place—by means of his word, so he meets them at the chosen place. There, he still refuses 'localization' on the Canaanite pattern—hence the requirement to destroy all the accoutrements of Canaanite religion—and the emphasis on his choice pre-empts any attempt to manipulate him on Israel's part. Yet his actual presence is achieved by his choice, implying as it does a giving of his presence that is conditioned by the people's reception of his word (v. 1), and by their response in worship.

The analogy between the two chapters can be taken further by an appeal here too to the idea of contingency. Deuteronomy 12 shares with ch. 4 an interest in time. Yahweh *has given* a land, and the people *shall be careful* to keep the commandments in it (12.1); again, 'you *shall not do* what we are doing *this day...*' (12.8). That ch. 12 is consciously on a time line of promise–fulfilment, like ch. 4, emerges from 12.20 ('as he has promised you'). Yet the fulfilment is not a necessary stopping-point; the possibility of the loss of everything that is given is contained in the warnings not to be ensnared by the practices of other nations, and the implied similarity between their fate and Israel's (12.30).

The importance of the analogy between Horeb and the chosen place appears from G. Millar's treatment of the theme of place in the framework (above). Horeb[128] gives way to Moab (though a rhetorical identity is established between the two places). That succession of place now extends to the 'chosen place' of the altar-law.

## Conclusions

I began the present essay by asking whether it was satisfying to think that Deuteronomy's refusal to name the place of the altar-law was merely intended to conform to the device of Mosaic authorship. Certain treatments, indeed, had gone beyond this, to look for positive significance in the terms of Deuteronomy 12, but had tended to think in

---

128. It may be that the name Horeb is preferred by Deuteronomy because in itself it seems to be non-specific about location, a 'waste-place', possibly intending thus to detract from the idea that even the 'mountain of God' *par excellence* had any intrinsic significance. See L. Perlitt, 'Horeb und Sinai', in *Beiträge* (ed. Donner *et al.*), pp. 303-22; Perlitt thinks the name is chosen out of a desire not to be too specific about location, though he goes too far when he argues that Horeb is no longer even thought of in Deuteronomy as a mountain (pp. 307-308).

terms of a compromise between conceptions of divine presence which were in reality uneasy bedfellows. Certain modern revivals of Wellhausen's view had thought of Deuteronomy as 'statist' because of its alleged centring of all of Israel's life on the royal–hierocratic synthesis of the Jerusalem cult. The view advocated here is in complete contrast. It seems to me that Deuteronomy's decision to refrain from naming a place is in keeping with its fundamental understanding of divine presence, which it consistently advocates. In that understanding lies a paradox. Yahweh really makes himself present among his people on earth, in the context of a relationship which he enters with them at a time and in a place. That commitment is realized, necessarily, in actual places. Herein, of course, is an affirmation of actual political and religious arrangements; Deuteronomy by no means abolishes the responsibility of Israel to weave and maintain the fabric of social and political life—quite the reverse. The significance, however, of any given arrangement (that is to say 'place' in its three-dimensional complexity) is not intrinsic; rather, it is entirely contingent (where contingency is given flesh by the Mosaic covenant). No place which becomes the object of Yahweh's choice takes on intrinsic significance, nor has it permanent status. This, I suggest, is what is entailed by the silence of Deuteronomy on the identity of the place. The formula of the altar-law encapsulates (not to say enshrines) the non-significance of individual places.

# CONCLUSION

We have undertaken a comprehensive study of the themes of time and place in Deuteronomy as a contribution to an understanding of the book's thought on the relationships between God and people, land and worship. The first part of the study (Millar) showed the importance of the motif of 'journey' in the parenesis of the 'framework'. This was complemented by a concept of time which allowed successive generations of Israel to stand again at 'Horeb', as it were, confronted by the challenge to enter and keep the covenant. Time and place are the axes of a covenant that is perpetually renewable.

Israel's life from its beginnings in Egypt was conceived as a series of crises in which its decision was crucial to its future survival. This ethical journey began with the flight from Egypt, and continued with the acceptance of the covenant at Horeb, the challenge to faith in Yahweh at Kadesh, and the invitation in Moab to accept his word as the way of life in the land. Yet while each decision is crucial, none is final, each pointing rather to yet others which lie in the future. The promised possession of the land, therefore, is perpetually contingent. The offer is made, importantly, from a point outside the land. And indeed, the possibility and reality of existence outside the land—at unspecified future times—is sharply portrayed, when Israel shows by its weakness a tendency to return to Egypt (Deut. 1.26-28; 9.22-24), and when Moses dies in Moab (1.37; 34.5-8).

The correlative of the ethical journey is Yahweh's manifestation of himself to Israel in his word. Within the journey rhetoric, Deuteronomy's understanding of the divine law is shaped. At the heart of Deuteronomy 1–11 is the Decalogue (5.1-21), preceded by the historical retrospect (vv. 1-3) and an 'overture' (4), and leading into sustained exhortation (5.22–11.32). The journey is shaped both by Yahweh's presence and by his expressed will. As Israel progresses from place to place, he is close to them along the way (immanent: 1.31; 4.7), yet also he speaks unseen from heaven (transcendent: 4.36; 5.22). The preservation of the divine distance even at moments of close encounter is a vital ingredient in a relationship that is not constituted by an unconditional guarantee, but must always be freshly realized.

The second part of the study (McConville) applied these results to the law code in general and the altar-law in particular. A historical investigation, from the Old Testament itself to modern criticism, showed that the altar-law had generally been interpreted not as a mere identifier of a place of worship, but for what it implied about the nature of the presence of God with Israel. This was true for the Deuteronomic History and various Jewish writings of the early post-biblical period. Despite obvious differences of interest, furthermore, there was a certain convergence in this respect between ancient and modern interpreters.

An exegetical study addressing topics of the divine name, the divine presence, and the intention of the place formula itself then led to an understanding of the law which echoed the contention that it had fundamentally to do with the nature of God's presence: God is really present with his people at the place which he chooses, though that presence is subject to their keeping the covenant; in giving his presence, therefore, he also maintains his freedom.

The concepts of presence and freedom were further articulated by a contextual study of the altar-law, in which the thought of Deuteronomy 12 was illuminated by a comparison with that of ch. 4, and the language of transcendence and immanence. In ch. 4 transcendence was expressed by the insistence that God was in heaven and invisible to human beings; his immanence could not be expressed by the making of idols, but was bound closely to the keeping of his commandments in the context of covenant faithfulness. In ch. 12, God's transcendence implied his freedom to choose the place of worship, while his immanence was expressed in his real presence at the sanctuary, together with the obligation of the people to meet him there in faithful worship.

The most far-reaching consequence of the interpretation which we have offered is the challenge which it presents to the view that Deuteronomy constituted the programme for Josiah's reform, in the sense of being a centralizing, 'statist' document. The reverse is the case. Deuteronomy, while it is certainly a mandate for political and practical action rightly conceived (that is, in covenant faithfulness), is no bulwark of the establishment. Its insistence on the provisionality of all 'present' arrangements stands firmly against this very concept. The people of Israel stand always 'before the LORD' at the place where he meets them, their destiny perpetually dependent on their decision about the covenant.

# BIBLIOGRAPHY

Albright, W.F., 'Some Remarks on the Song of Moses in Deut xxxii', *VT* 9 (1959), pp. 339-46.

Allen, L., *Psalms 101–150* (WBC; Waco, TX: Word, 1983).

Alt, A., 'The Origin of OT Law', in *Essays on Old Testament History and Religion* (ET Oxford: Blackwell, 1966).

Anbar, M., 'The Story of the Building of an Altar on Mount Ebal', in *Das Deuteronomium* (ed. N. Lohfink, *q.v.*), pp. 304-10.

Andersen, F.I., and D.N. Freedman, *Amos* (AB; New York: Doubleday, 1989).

Bächli, O., *Israel und die Völker* (Zürich: Zwingli Verlag, 1962).

Baltzer, K., *The Covenant Formulary* (Oxford: Oxford University Press, 1970).

Barr, J., 'Theophany and Anthropomorphism in the Old Testament', in *Congress Volume, Oxford 1959* (ed. J.A. Emerton *et al.*; VTSup, 7; Leiden: Brill, 1959), pp. 31-38.

Bartlett, J.R., 'Sihon and Og, Kings of the Amorites', *VT* 20 (1970), pp. 257-77.

Barth, K., *Church Dogmatics* II.1. *The Doctrine of God* (Edinburgh: T. & T. Clark, 1957).

Baumann, E., 'Das Lied Moses auf seine gedankliche Geschlossenheit untersucht', *VT* 6 (1956), pp. 414-24.

Bellefontaine, E., 'The Curses of Deuteronomy 27: Their Relationship to the Prohibitives', in *No Famine in the Land: Studies in Honor of J.L. McKenzie* (ed. W. Flanagan and A.W. Robinson; Missoula: Scholars Press, 1975), pp. 49-61.

Berg, S.B., *The Book of Esther: Motifs, Themes and Structures* (Missoula: Scholars Press, 1979).

Blair, E.P., 'An Appeal to Remembrance: The Memory Motif in Deuteronomy', *Int* 15 (1961), pp. 41-47.

Boston, J.R., 'The Wisdom Influence upon the Song of Moses', *JBL* 87 (1968), pp. 166-78.

Braulik, G., 'Die Ausdrücke für Gesetz im Buch Deuteronomium', *Bib* 51 (1970), pp. 39-66.

—'Weisheit, Gottesnähe und Gesetz—Zum Kerygma von Deuteronomium 4,5-8', in *Studien zum Pentateuch* (FS W. Kornfeld; ed. G. Braulik; Vienna: Herder & Herder, 1977), pp. 165-95, reprinted in *Studien zur Theologie des Deuteronomiums* (Stuttgarter Biblische Aufsatzbände, Altes Testament, 2; Stuttgart: Katholisches Bibelwerk, 1988), pp. 53-93.

—Review of Mittmann, *Deuteronomium 1:1–6:3 Literarkritisch und traditionsgeschichtlich untersucht*, by S. Mittmann, *Bib* 59 (1978), pp. 351-83.

—*Die Mittel deuteronomischer Rhetorik erhoben aus Deuteronomium 4,1-40* (AnBib, 68; Rome: Pontifical Biblical Institute, 1978).

—'Die Abfolge der Gesetze in Deuteronomium 12–26 und der Dekalog', in *Das Deuteronomium* (ed. N. Lohfink, *q.v.*), pp. 252-72.

—*Die deuteronomischen Gesetze und der Dekalog* (SBS, 145; Stuttgart: Katholisches Bibelwerk, 1991).

Brekelmans, C., 'Deuteronomy 5', in *Das Deuteronomium* (ed. N. Lohfink, *q.v.*), pp. 164-73.

Brooke G.J. (ed.), *Temple Scroll Studies* (JSPSup, 7; Sheffield: JSOT Press, 1989).

Brown, R., *The Message of Deuteronomy* (Leicester: IVP, 1993).

Bruce, F.F., *The Book of Acts* (NICNT; Grand Rapids: Eerdmans, 1954).

Brueggemann, W., *The Land* (OBT; Philadelphia: Fortress, 1977).

—'Imagination as a Mode of Fidelity', in *Understanding the Word: Essays in Honour of B.W. Anderson* (ed. J.T. Butler, E.W. Conrad and B.C. Ollen burger; JSOTSup, 37; Sheffield: JSOT Press, 1985), pp. 1-27.

Bülow, S., 'Der Berg des Fluches', *ZDPV* 73 (1957), pp. 100-107.

Cazelles, H., 'Passages in the Singular within Discourses in the Plural of Dt. 1–4', *CBQ* 29 (1967), pp. 207-19.

Charlesworth, H. (ed.), *The Old Testament Pseudepigrapha* (2 vols.; New York: Doubleday, 1985).

Chilton, B.D., *The Glory of Israel: The Theology and Provenience of the Isaiah Targum* (Sheffield: JSOT Press, 1983).

Christensen, D.L., 'Form and Structure in Deuteronomy 1–11', in *Das Deuteronomium* (ed. Lohfink, *q.v.*), pp. 135-44.

—*Deuteronomy 1–11* (WBC; Dallas: Word, 1991).

Clements, R.E., 'Deuteronomy and the Jerusalem Cult Tradition', *VT* 15 (1965), pp. 300-12.

Coats, G.W., 'Conquest Traditions in the Wilderness Theme', *JBL* 95 (1976), pp. 177-90.

—'Legendary Elements in the Moses Death Reports', *CBQ* 39 (1977), pp. 34-44.

Craigie, P.C., *The Book of Deuteronomy* (NICOT; Grand Rapids: Eerdmans, 1976).

Cross, F.M., *Canaanite Myth and Hebrew Epic* (Cambridge, MA: Harvard University Press, 1973).

Vries, S.J. de, *Yesterday, Today and Tomorrow: Time and History in the Old Testament* (Grand Rapids: Eerdmans, 1975).

Dion, P.E., 'Deuteronomy 13: The Suppression of Alien Religious Propaganda during the Late Monarchical Era', in *Law and Ideology in Monarchic Israel* (ed. Halpern and Hobson, *q.v.*), pp. 147-216.

Dogniez, C., and M. Harl, *Le Deutéronome* (La Bible d'Alexandrie, 5; Paris: Les Editions du Cerf, 1992).

Drazin, I., *Targum Onkelos to Deuteronomy* (New York: Ktav, 1982).

Driver, S.R., *A Critical and Exegetical Commentary on Deuteronomy* (ICC; Edinburgh: T. & T. Clark, 3rd edn, 1901).

Dumermuth, F., 'Zur deuteronomischen Kulttheologie und ihren Voraussetzungen', *ZAW* 70 (1958), pp. 59-98.

Eissfeldt, O., 'Silo und Jerusalem', in *Congress Volume, Strasbourg 1956* (ed. J.A. Emerton *et al.*; VTSup, 4; Leiden: Brill, 1956), pp. 138-48.

—*Das Lied Moses* (Berichte über die Verhandlung der Sächsischen Akademie der Wissenschaften zu Leipzig, 104/5; 1958).

Flanagan, W., and A.W. Robinson (eds.), *No Famine in the Land* (FS J.L. McKenzie; Missoula: Scholars Press, 1976).

Fowler, M.D., 'The Meaning of *lipnê YHWH* in the Old Testament', *ZAW* 99 (1987), pp. 384-90.

Goldberg, M., *Untersuchungen über die Vorstellung von der Schekhinah in der frühen rabbinischen Literatur* (SJ, 5; Berlin: de Gruyter, 1969).

Grossfeld, B., *Targum Onqelos to Deuteronomy* (Edinburgh: T. & T. Clark, 1988).

Halbe, J., 'Gemeinschaft die Welt unterbricht', in *Das Deuteronomium* (ed. Lohfink, *q.v.*), pp. 55-75.

Halpern, B., 'The Centralisation Formula in Deuteronomy', *VT* 31 (1981), pp. 20-38.

—'Jerusalem and the Lineages in the Seventh Century BCE: Kinship and the Rise of Individual Moral Liability', in *Law and Ideology in Monarchic Israel* (ed. Halpern and Hobson, *q.v.*), pp. 11-107.

Halpern, B., and D. Hobson (eds.), *Law and Ideology in Monarchic Israel* (JSOTSup, 124; Sheffield: JSOT Press, 1991).

Hanson, P.D., *The Dawn of Apocalyptic* (Philadelphia: Fortress Press, 1975).

Hempel, J., *Die Schichten des Deuteronomium* (Leipzig: Voigtländer, 1914).

Hillers, D.R., *Treaty Curses and the Old Testament Prophets* (BibOr 16; Rome: Pontifical Biblical Institute, 1964).

Jenson, P.P., *Graded Holiness* (JSOTSup, 106; Sheffield: JSOT Press, 1992).

Jones, D.R., *Jeremiah* (NCB; London: Marshall Pickering, 1992).

Kaufman, S.A., 'The Structure of the Deuteronomic Law', *Maarav* 1/2 (1979), pp. 105-58.

Keil, C.F., *Deuteronomy*, in C.F. Keil and F. Delitzsch, *Commentary on the Old Testament*. I. *The Pentateuch* ET 1864; repr. Grand Rapids: Eerdmans, 1988).

Kleinert, P., *Untersuchungen zur alttestamentlichen Rechts- und Literaturgeschichte*. I. *Das Deuteronomium und der Deuteronomiker* (Leipzig: Velhagen & Klasing, 1872).

Knapp, D., *Deuteronomium 4: Literarische Analyse und theologische Interpretation* (Göttingen: Vandenhoeck & Ruprecht, 1987).

Laberge, L., 'Le lieu que YHWH a choisi pour y mettre son Nom: (TM, LXX, Vg, et Targums). Contribution à la critique textuelle d'une formule deutéronomiste', *EstBib* 43 (1985), pp. 209-36.

Lewy, I., 'The Puzzle of Deuteronomy 27', *VT* 12 (1962), pp. 207-11.

Lohfink, N., 'Darstellungskunst und Theologie in Dtn. 1:6–3:2', *Bib* 41 (1960), pp. 105-34.

—'Der Bundesschluss im Land Moab: Redaktiongeschichtliches zu Dt 28,69–32,47', *BZ* NF 6 (1962), pp. 32-56.

—'Die deuteronomische Darstellung des Übergangs der Führung Israels von Moses auf Josue', *Scholastik* 37 (1962), pp. 32-44, reprinted in *idem*, *Studien zum Deuteronomium*, pp. 83-97.

—*Das Hauptgebot: Eine Untersuchung literarischer Einleitungsfragen zu Dtn. 5–11* (AnBib 20; Rome: Pontifical Biblical Institute, 1963).

—'Die Bundesurkunde des Königs Josias', *Bib* 44 (1963), pp. 261-88, 461-98.

—'Verkündigung des Hauptgebots in der jüngsten Schicht des Deuteronomiums', originally in *Bibel und Leben* 5 (1964), and in a modified form as 'Höre, Israel! Auslegung von Texten aus dem Buch Deuteronomium', *Die Welt der Bibel* 18 (1965), reprinted in *idem*, *Studien zum Deuteronomium*, pp. 167-92.

—Review of *Literarkritische, formgeschichtliche und stilkritische Untersuchungen zum Deuteronomium*, by J. Plöger,*Bib* 49 (1968), pp. 110-15.

—*Das Deuteronomium* (BETL, 68; Leuven: Leuven University Press, 1985).

—'Die *"huqqîm umispātîm"* im Buch Deuteronomium und ihre Neubegrenzung durch Dtn. 12:1', *Bib* 70 (1989), pp. 1-27.

—*Studien zum Deuteronomium und zur Deuteronomischen Literatur*, I (Stuttgarter Biblische Aufsatzbände, Altes Testament, 8; Stuttgart: Katholisches Bibelwerk, 1990).

Lopez, F.G., 'Analyse littéraire de Deut. 5–11', *RB* 84 (1977), pp. 481-522 and 85 (1978), pp. 1-49.

Maier, J., *The Temple Scroll* (JSTSup, 34; Sheffield: JSOT Press, 1985).

Manson, W., *The Epistle to the Hebrews* (London: Hodder & Stoughton, 1951).

Mayes, A.D.H., *Deuteronomy* (NCB; Grand Rapids: Eerdmans; London: Marshall, Morgan & Scott, 1979).

McConville, J.G., 'God's Name and God's Glory', *TynBul* 30 (1979), pp. 149-63.

—*Law and Theology in Deuteronomy* (JSOTSup, 33; Sheffield: JSOT Press, 1984).

—'Narrative and Meaning in the Books of Kings', *Bib* 70 (1989), pp. 31-49.

—'1 Kings viii 46-53 and the Deuteronomic Hope', *VT* 42 (1992), pp. 67-79.

—'Jerusalem in the Old Testament', in *Jerusalem Past and Present* (ed. P.W.L. Walker; Cambridge: Tyndale House, 1992), pp. 21-51.

—*Grace in the End: A Study in Deuteronomic Theology* (Carlisle: Paternoster, 1993).

—*Judgment and Promise: An Interpretation of the Book of Jeremiah* (Leicester: Apollos; Winona Lake: Eisenbrauns, 1993).

Mendenhall, G.E., 'Samuel's Broken *Rib*: Deut. 32', in *No Famine in the Land* (ed. W. Flanagan and W. Robinson, *q.v.*).

Merendino, R.P., *Das Deuteronomische Gesetz* (BBB, 31; Bonn: Peter Hanstein, 1969).

Mettinger, T.N.D., *The Dethronement of Sabaoth: Studies in the Shem and Kabod Theologies* (ConBOT, 18; Lund: CWK Gleerup, 1982).

Millar, J.G., *The Ethics of Deuteronomy* (DPhil dissertation Oxford University, forthcoming).

Miller, P.D., *Deuteronomy* (Interpretation; Louisville: John Knox Press, 1990).

Minette de Tillesse, G., 'Sections "Tu" et Sections "Vous" dans le Deutéronome', *VT* 12 (1982), pp. 29-87.

Mittmann, S., *Deuteronomium 1:1–6:3 Literarkritisch und traditionsgeschichtlich untersucht* (BZAW, 39; Berlin: A. Töpelmann, 1975).

Moran, W.L., 'The End of the Unholy War and the Anti-Exodus', *Bib* 44 (1963), pp. 333-42.

Neusner, J., *Sifre to Deuteronomy*, I, II BJS, 98, 101; Atlanta: Scholars Press, 1987).

Nicholson, E.W., *Deuteronomy and Tradition* (Oxford: Blackwell, 1967).

—'The Decalogue as the Direct Address of God', *VT* 27 (1977), pp. 422-33.

—*God and his People* (Oxford: Clarendon, 1986).

Nickelsburg, G.W.E., *Jewish Literature between the Bible and the Mishnah* (London: SCM Press, 1981).

Niehaus, J.J., 'The Central Sanctuary: Where and When?', *TynBul* 43.1 (1992), pp. 3-30.

Noth, M., *Leviticus* (OTL; London: SCM Press, 1965).

—*The Deuteronomistic History* (JSOTSup, 15; Sheffield: JSOT Press, 2nd edn, 1981), ET of Part I of *Überlieferungsgeschichtliche Studien* (2nd edn, Tübingen: Max Niemeyer, 1957).

Paul, M.J. *Het Archimedisch Punt van de Pentateuchkritik* ('s-Gravenhage: Boekencentrum, 1988).

Perlitt, L., 'Horeb und Sinai', in *Beiträge zur alttestamentliche Theologie* (FS W. Zimmerli; ed. H. Donner *et al*; Göttingen; Vandenhoeck & Ruprecht, 1977), pp. 303-22.

—'Deuteronomium 1–3 im Streit der exegetischen Methoden', in *Das Deuteronomium* (ed. N. Lohfink, *q.v.*), pp. 149-63.

Plöger, J.G., *Literarkritische, formgeschichtliche und stilkritische Untersuchungen zum Deuteronomium* (BBB, 26: Bonn: Peter Hanstein, 1967).

Polzin, R., *Moses and the Deuteronomist* (New York: Seabury, 1980).

Preuss, H.D., *Deuteronomium* (Erträge der Forschung, 164; Darmstadt: Wissenschaftliche Buchgesellschaft, 1988).

Rad, G. von, 'Zelt und Lade', *NKZ* 42 (1931), pp. 476-98 (= 'The Tent and the Ark', in *idem*, *The Problem of the Hexateuch*, pp. 103-24.

—*Studies in Deuteronomy* (London: SCM Press, 1953).

—*Deuteronomy* (OTL; London: SCM Press, 1966).

—*The Problem of the Hexateuch and other Essays* (ET London: SCM Press, 1984 [repr. 1966]).

Robertson, D.A., *Linguistic Evidence in Dating Early Hebrew Poetry* (SBLDS, 3; Missoula: Scholars Press, 1972).

Rofé, A., 'The Covenant in the Land of Moab Dt 28:69–30:20', in *Das Deuteronomium* (ed. N. Lohfink, *q.v.*), pp. 310-20.

Rose, M., *Der Ausschliesslichkeitsanspruch Jahwes* (BWANT, 106; Stuttgart: Kohlhammer, 1975).

Rosenbaum, M., and A.M. Silbermann, *Pentateuch with Targum Onkelos, Haphtaroth and Prayers for Sabbath, and Rashi's Commentary: Deuteronomy* (London: Shapiro, Vallentine & Co., 1934).

Rost, L., 'Die Bezeichnungen für Land und Volk', in *Das Kleine Credo und andere Studien zum Alten Testament* (Heidelberg: Quelle & Meyer, 1965), pp. 76-101.

Rowley, H.H., *Worship in Ancient Israel* (London: SPCK, 1967).

Schottroff, W., *Der altisraelitische Fluchspruch* (WMANT, 30; Neukirchen: Neukirchener Verlag, 1969).

Schulz, H., *Das Todesrecht im Alten Testament* (BZAW, 114; Berlin: A. Töpelmann, 1969).

Seeligmann, I., 'Erkenntnis Gottes und historisches Bewusstsein im alten Israel', in *Beiträge zur Alttestamentlichen Theologie* (FS W. Zimmerli; ed. H. Donner *et al.*; Göttingen: Vandenhoeck & Ruprecht, 1977), pp. 414-45.

Seitz, G., *Redaktionsgeschichtliche Studien zum Deuteronomium* (BWANT, 93; Stuttgart: Kohlhammer, 1971).

Smith, G.A., *The Historical Geography of the Holy Land* (London: Hodder & Stoughton, 25th edn, 1931).

Stegemann, H., 'The Literary Composition of the Temple Scroll and its Status at Qumran', in *Temple Scroll Studies* (ed. G.J. Brooke, *q.v.*), pp. 123-48.

Sumner, W.A., 'Israel's encounters with Edom, Moab, Ammon, Sihon and Og according to the Deuteronomist', *VT* 18 (1968), pp. 216-28.

Thompson, J.A., *Deuteronomy* (TOTC; Leicester: IVP, 1974).

Van Seters, J., 'The Conquest of Sihon's Kingdom: A Literary Examination', *JBL* 91 (1972), pp. 182-97.

Vaux, R. de, 'Le lieu que Yahvé a choisi pour y établir son nom', in *Das Ferne und Nahe Wort* (FS L. Rost; ed. F. Maas; BZAW, 105; Gresseu: Töpelmann, 1967), pp. 219-28.

Vermeylen, J., 'Les sections narratives de Deut 5–11 et leur relation à Ex 19–34', in *Das Deuteronomium* (ed. Lohfink, *q.v.*), pp. 174-207.

Waldow, H.E. von, 'Israel and her Land: Some Theological Considerations', in *A Light Unto My Path: Old Testament Studies in Honour of J.M. Myers* (ed. H. Bream; Philadelphia: Temple University Press, 1974), pp.493-508.

Waltke, B., and M. O'Connor,, *Biblical Hebrew Syntax* (Winona Lake: Eisenbrauns, 1990).

Weinfeld, M., *Deuteronomy and the Deuteronomic School* (Oxford: Clarendon, 1972).

—'The Emergence of the Deuteronomic Movement: The Historical Antecedents', in *Das Deuteronomium* (ed. Lohfink, *q.v.*), pp. 76-98.

—*Deuteronomy 1–11* (AB; New York: Doubleday, 1990).

Wellhausen, J., *Prolegomena to the History of Ancient Israel* (Edinburgh: A. & C. Black, 1885).

Wenham, G.J., 'Deuteronomy and the Central Sanctuary', *TynBul* 22 (1971), pp. 103-18.

—*Numbers* (TOTC; Leicester: IVP, 1981).

Westermann, C., *Grundformen prophetischer Rede* (BEvT, 31; Munich: Chr. Kaiser Verlag, 1964).

Wette, W.M.L. de, *Dissertatio critica-exegetica qua Deuteronomium a prioribus Pentateuchi Libris diversum, alius cuiusdam recentioris auctoris opus esse monstratur* (Jena, 1805).

Williamson, H.G.M., 'Eschatology in Chronicles', *TB* 28 (1977), pp. 115-54.

—*Ezra–Nehemiah* (WBC; Waco, TX: Word, 1985).

Wilson, R.R., *Prophecy in Ancient Israel* (Philadelphia: Fortress Press, 1980).

Wilson, I., 'Divine Presence in Deuteronomy' (PhD thesis, Cambridge University, 1992).

Wise, M.O., *A Critical Study of the Temple Scroll from Qumran Cave 11* (Chicago: University of Chicago Press, 1990).

Wright, G.E., 'The Lawsuit of God', in *Israel's Prophetic Heritage* (FS J. Muilenburg; ed. B.W. Anderson and W. Harrelson; London: SCM Press, 1962), pp. 26-67.

## INDEX OF AUTHORS